starting *from* scratch

D1372295

372.136
LEV

starting *from* scratch

one classroom builds its own curriculum

steven levy

Heinemann ♥ Portsmouth, NH

DISCARD - WEEDED

Heinemann
A division of Reed Elsevier Inc.
361 Hanover Street
Portsmouth, NH 03801–3912

Offices and agents throughout the world

© 1996 by Steven Levy

All rights reserved. No part of this book may be reproduced in any form or by
any electronic or mechanical means, including information storage and retrieval
systems, without permission in writing from the publisher, except by a reviewer,
who may quote brief passages in a review.

A version of Chapter 3 was published as *Something from Nothing: A Fourth Grade
Expedition into Economy, Community, and History.* Learning Expeditions: Studies
from the Field Monograph Series, no. 3. Cambridge, Mass.: Expeditionary
Learning Outward Bound®, 1994.

Library of Congress Cataloging-in-Publication Data
Levy, Steven, 1949–
Starting from scratch : one classroom builds its own curriculum / Steven Levy.
p.   cm.
Includes bibliographical references.
ISBN 0-435-07205-6(alk. paper)
1. Project method in teaching—United States.   2. Active learning—United States.
3. American history—Study and teaching (Elementary)   4. Education,
Elementary—United States—Curricula.   I. Title.
LB1027.43.L19   1996
372.13'6—dc20
96-4126
CIP

Editor: Carolyn Coman
Production: Vicki Kasabian
Book and cover design: Jenny Jensen Greenleaf
Manufacturing: Louise Richardson

Printed in the United States of America on acid-free paper
99 98 97 96 EB 1 2 3 4 5

Dedication

I was in Washington, D.C., recently, one of thirty-six teachers being honored by the Walt Disney company. An outstanding moment of the week was our visit to the Tomb of the Unknown Soldier. Being one of several hundred people standing in rapt attention for thirty minutes as a soldier took twenty-two steps back and forth across a narrow runway was unforgettable. We were spellbound by the precise movements of the soldier and in awe of a sacrifice greater than any of us had been called to bear.

Standing there I couldn't help but think of all the unknown teachers across our land who go to work every day, hardly noticed, rarely appreciated, dedicating their lives to our children, our future. I imagined a monument to recognize and honor the unknown teacher. Inscribed at the base might be the words of Frederick Douglass to Harriet Tubman (I have substituted *children* for *bondmen and women*):

> You ask for what you do not need when you call on me for a word of commendation. I need such words from you far more than you can need them from me. . . . Most that I have done and suffered in the service of our cause has been in public, and I have received much encouragement every step of the way. You, on the other hand have labored in a private way. I have wrought in the day, you in the night. I have had the applause of the crowd and the satisfaction of being approved by the multitude, while the most that you have done has been witnessed by a few trembling [children], whose

heartfelt "God bless you" has been your only reward. The midnight sky and the silent stars have been the witnesses of your devotion and your heroism.

I dedicate this book to the unknown teachers who guide and inspire children on their way toward freedom. Let it give witnessing eyes to the midnight sky and applauding hands to the silent stars.

Contents

Acknowledgments

Somewhere in every teacher's storehouse are vast archives of ideas and activities "stolen" from other teachers. Every thought in this book can probably be traced to an inspiration born of conversations with many colleagues and mentors. Like all teachers, I take a thought from one, an activity from another, materials from a third, and weave them together in different ways to meet the needs of my students. I am grateful to the many teachers who have allowed me to build on their ideas and work.

I thank John F. Gardner, former director of the Waldorf Institute at Adelphi University, who had a profound influence in shaping my understanding of children and the world. I thank the teachers at the Waldorf School in Lexington, Massachusetts, with whom I labored for many years to manifest our ideals in the reality of our classrooms. I thank my fellow teachers at Bowman School, who have tolerated my eccentricities and supported me in times of struggle and triumph. I am grateful to the administrators of the Lexington Public Schools for giving me room to develop my own teaching style, especially Dave Horton, former principal at Bowman School, who took a chance in hiring me and continues to encourage me in my career. I thank Cathy Morocco, Bridget Dalton, Penny Rawson, Maureen Riley, and others at the Education Development Center in Newton who gave me an opportunity to reflect with them about how children learn. I thank my colleagues at ATLAS (Authentic Teaching and Learning for All Students) for inviting me to join the "conversations," especially Shari

Robinson and Marielle Palombo, who helped me think about ways to share what I have learned about teaching with other teachers, and Sid Smith, who introduced me to the concept *push*. Sid's probing questions helped me articulate many of the methods and strategies I didn't even know I used. Likewise, Bethany Rogers, from the Coalition of Essential Schools, crafted sharp and lucid critiques, helping me to develop my "argument." I thank my friends at Expeditionary Learning, especially Leah Rugen, for recognizing the writer in me and helping to develop it. Special thanks to Anthony Valenti, who helped me to find my "voice" and to choose the right words to say what I really meant, and Carolyn Coman, my editor at Heinemann, a constant source of guidance and encouragement. I also thank Alan Huisman at Heinemann who, in so many cases, knew better than I what I was trying to say.

I am grateful to the many parents who have entrusted their children to me over the years. Several have been instrumental in helping me share my work with a broader audience: Debbie Neumann, who convinced me I had something to say that might be useful to other teachers and, as my first editor, sharpened my attention to the subtle precision of our language; Terri Butler, who left me the lasting treasure of a video that recorded the work of an entire year; Peggy Stevens, who saw the video's potential for helping teachers; and Elizabeth Westling, who has been of inestimable value both inside and outside the classroom. I am especially grateful to the children in my classes, whose consistently outstanding work has caused me to look good as their teacher.

I thank my wife, Joanna, who reminds me of my real priorities (God and family both come before work), and my children, Noah, Mariam, Susannah, and Naomi, who more than anyone have prepared my heart with the compassion I need to be a loving teacher. I thank my father, who taught me I could be anything I wanted and then was proud when I chose to be a teacher, and my mother, who taught me always to say thank you.

I thank the readers of this book in advance, for giving your time to consider these thoughts and, I hope, develop them further in your own work.

Finally, I realize that the talents I have as a teacher are gifts from God, to whom my gratitude is unceasing.

Introduction

No profession is more public than teaching. Every move a teacher makes is scrutinized, every word examined, every decision challenged. On the other hand, teaching is perhaps also the most private profession. A teacher accomplishes so much that no one is there to witness.

This was brought home one morning when, after a sleepless night, I rose before dawn and decided to play a round of golf before my first class. The sky was dark when I arrived at Pine Meadows Golf Club. The morning dew still glistened on the fairways.

The sun was just visible over the trees as I reached the par three sixth hole. I hit a four iron and watched the ball sail toward the green. It looked right on target, but when I approached the green I couldn't find the ball anywhere. After combing the long grass in front of the green and searching the woods behind it, I decided to play another ball. But as I lined up the shot, I noticed a small, round, green indentation in the white dew that still covered the green. About two feet away was another. Then another, a foot away; then six inches; then the indentation gradually transformed into a line that I followed with amazement as it disappeared into the hole. I had sunk a hole in one. Immediately a question plagued what should have been my unmitigated joy: is a hole in one really a hole in one if no one is there to see it?

I could not do what I always did when the ball went into the hole: just take it out. That seemed much too plebeian a gesture for such a magnificent moment. Besides, it would definitely end my chances of finding a witness. On the other hand, if I left it there, the next golfer to come along would surely attribute it to some senile duffer who forgot to retrieve his ball after sinking the third or fourth putt. Mercifully, I heard the drone of a tractor grooming the fairway several holes away. I ran over and begged the driver to come and watch as I took the ball out of the hole. "Sure, buddy," he condescended, then drove reluctantly over to the sixth green. I pointed out that there were no footprints on the green and showed him the fading trail the ball had left to reveal the path of my lonesome glory. I ceremoniously retrieved the ball and thanked him for his kindness as he muttered something under his breath and rode quickly back to work.

I did not tell anyone at school that day about my experience. But a week later we were asked to bring something to a faculty meeting that had significant personal value. Not having thought much about the assignment before the meeting, I grabbed a golf ball on my way to school. I thought I would tell the story of the hole in one.

The meeting was more intimate and personal than any we had ever shared. Teachers told stories of lost loved ones, of turning points in life, of miraculous healings and recoveries. People were talking about life and death and I had a golf ball in my hand! It wasn't until after the meeting that I realized the hole in one was the perfect story to share at a faculty meeting. It represented exactly the loneliness a teacher feels in the classroom. No one is there to see the outstanding "shots" we make in our classroom: when we introduce Tanya to the hidden meaning of the letter M, when we coax the first "I'm sorry" Charles has ever said, when we teach percentages and the class breaks into a spontaneous Aha!

Teachers feel the world would be a better place if someone were there to watch these "holes in one." The children are there, of course, but they cannot appreciate the hours of work that brought clarity to that lesson, the luminous insight that brought peace to a chronic conflict, the gentle word that brought hope to a desperate child. I wrote this book in part to reveal some of the "holes-in-one" that have occurred behind one classroom door.

Another reason for writing this book was to demonstrate a way to reconcile conflicts that have recently been the subject of much debate in our schools and communities. Project-based learning squares off against basic skills. Integrated curriculum wrestles with discipline-centered instruction. State and national frameworks and mandates compete with local and individual interests and initiatives. I believe it is possible to teach basic skills in the course of exciting and relevant projects, to master the methods and content of specific disciplines through an integrated curriculum, and to connect students' interests and questions to the frameworks designed by the state. The examples described in this book will demonstrate some of the ways these issues might be addressed.

I first became interested in education for monetary reasons. It's true. While sweating at my job in a dark warehouse near the banks of the Mississippi River the summer after my sophomore year at Colgate University, I wondered if there wasn't some other way I could make the money I needed for college. Although I did not have any experience working with children, I had an idea of starting a summer camp. I knew many families in my hometown of University City, Missouri, and wondered if I could convince a few parents to entrust me with their children. I could take them to a different place—the art museum, the zoo, the country—each day. It sounded much more appealing than moving boxes around in the warehouse.

The next summer I organized the camp and found eight brave nine- and ten-year-old children to enroll. I loved the enthusiasm of those campers. They had a transforming, imaginative power that was able to turn disappointment into adventure. When we went to the museum and found it was closed, they created Olympic contests using the hickory nuts and branches on the adjacent grounds. When it rained during our trip to the country, they made leaf boats and sailed them down the rivulets. The seed of my becoming a teacher was planted that summer.

Over the next two summers I expanded the camp, inviting several friends to join me as counselors. We rented space above an art gallery and then from a fraternity at Washington University.

After I graduated from college I found a job at an urban high school outside of St. Louis. I had no educational training, but it was a desperate school, and they had some extra money from the federal government. Everyone at this school—students, teachers, administrators—all hated being there. I was hired to direct special projects with small groups of children. I thought my warmth and support would help them overcome the overwhelming obstacles in their environment, my encouragement and understanding would empower them to achieve their full potential. I listened sensitively to their stories and designed activities based on their interests.

I got clobbered. The students took complete advantage of my naïveté, using me to get whatever they wanted, which generally meant skipping classes. I signed permission slips to excuse one group of students from class because they had something important to talk to me about and they just left the building. I was making a film about the school with another group and they stole my camera. By the end of the year I asked to be assigned to the attendance office, where I made Xs every morning in a big black book. Every X was perfectly crafted, and the numbers marking the dates at the tops of the columns were elegant. It was surely the most artistic attendance book ever created, but I didn't see much future in it.

Two good things did come from my first teaching experience. First, I thought if I was going to be a teacher I had better take some time to study education. I began to look into the possibilities of attending graduate school. Second, the guidance counselor at the school gave me about forty acres of land for the camp. He had always wanted to run a summer camp and when he heard about my camp he thought the land would be a perfect place for it.

The next year I enrolled in a master's degree program at Adelphi University; classes were taught jointly by professors from the university and by teachers from a school on campus, the Waldorf School. The next summer I ran a sleepover camp in the foothills of the Ozarks between Doe Run and Knob Lick, Missouri.

My intention throughout graduate school was to return to Missouri and open a camp where students from the city could spend a week of refreshment and adventure in nature. However, in the spring before graduation I visited a small Waldorf nursery school in Cambridge, Massachusetts, that was looking for someone who could teach kindergarten and help build the school into a full elementary program. I was captivated by the thought of venturing away from my hometown and enticed by the attractions of the Boston area. Most of all, I was excited by the idea of being able to help shape a school from the beginning. I thought that if I could be part of creating the school, then I would not have to inherit the mistakes that were so apparent in all the other schools I saw.

Instead of inheriting others' mistakes, I got to make them all myself. That is a good thing, because lessons learned from experience are not easily forgotten. We did build a full school, kindergarten through eighth grade, and I taught every grade over the thirteen years I was there. In Waldorf schools one teacher stays with the same class of children from first through eighth grade. This structure allowed me an opportunity to see children develop over a period of time and also trained me in the practice of designing new curriculum every year. (I still feel guilty, as if I am cheating, if I do the same thing from one year to the next.)

Since leaving the Waldorf School in 1987, I have been teaching fourth grade at the Bowman School in Lexington, Massachusetts. For the past two years I have taught half time, sharing my class with another teacher. I spend the other half of my time consulting and conducting workshops for teachers.

Teachers, when not in the classroom, are generally in a constant state of either preparation or recovery. We do not usually take time to reflect. Writing this book has compelled me to do so, and the process has been extremely valuable for several reasons. Among the most beneficial results of bringing my instincts into consciousness is that I am able to engage in conversations with others about my approach to teaching. I can receive useful suggestions and critiques. I have also become aware of areas in my teaching that I have neglected or failed to think through. Thus, reflection and the writing it produces have become a valuable catalyst for my own professional development. This book is my attempt to make sense of my teaching experience and unpack the underlying strategies and perspectives that have guided my work.

My goal in teaching is to create an environment built on natural inquiry where students engage in real problems instead of worksheets and original research instead of textbooks. Active performances and meaningful products replace paper-and-pencil tests, and excellence is pursued in every detail. I fill my room with a rich variety of activities that allow the genius in each child to be expressed and developed. My class is a tapestry of questions, research, thinking, problem solving, music, poetry, drama, crafts, arts, and games, all integrated in a theme woven anew every year from threads of the children's natural wonder. We often find these themes in common objects in our environment. A grain of wheat, a strand of wool, the shoes we wear, and the name of our town have all led to exciting learning projects. I feel a special call to mine the extraordinary out of the everyday. Familiar objects that the children take for granted are filled with intrigue and meaning when we explore their origins. One can start with almost any object or idea and, through questioning, reflecting, and imagining, see through it like a window into the depth and breadth of the world. The fundamental principle is to set learning in the context of reality, where children need to develop knowledge and skills to make decisions or complete tasks relevant to their lives.

In the first two chapters, I reflect on the kind of teaching I think is important in meeting the needs of our children, inspiring us in our roles as teachers, and enlivening the curriculum we are responsible for teaching; I try to discern the principles and questions that guide me in the classroom. Chapter 3 describes a yearlong project that in many ways represents the culmination of what I have striven for twenty years to create in my classroom. "What Is the Ideal Classroom?" is my most complete attempt at setting high expectations, giving the students responsibility for their own learning, and involving the community in the schools. Chapters 4 through 9 describe various projects that illustrate different aspects of my teaching principles in action. I believe these examples are the most important part of the book, because they provide a detailed glimpse into the planning, thinking, and unfolding of a learning process that masters basic skills in the course of exciting adventures. We can find numerous guidelines for effective teaching in a variety of books and articles, but it is not so easy to find examples of what these principles look like when they are applied in the classroom. The final two chapters deal with character, discipline, and the challenge of educating students to become confident individuals who have a strong sense of belonging to a community.

The more I thought about what really counts in my teaching, the more I realized that asking the right questions is at its heart. There are many kinds of questions that can lead us into authentic curriculum, and they arise from a variety of sources in the classroom. Some questions are grand, essential inquiries that deal with broad and deep themes: What did John Adams mean when he wrote "The American Revolution was completed before the war commenced"? Other questions are more familiar, recovering the extraordinary in the everyday: Where does our bread come from? Where do our clothes come from? are two questions that have inspired challenging projects in my classes. Some questions arise in the process of studying areas of required curriculum: Where did our town get its name? My favorite questions are ones that arise from the natural activity of people coming together and sharing their experience. Once a child brought in his baseball card collection, which surprisingly led us to the question, Why does America, foremost manufacturer in the world, wear shoes made on the other side of the earth? (I explain how we got there in Chapter 5.) Sometimes I ask questions that are imaginative but that require a thoughtful and reasoned response. Which is the greatest number? led us into an imaginative exploration of the qualities of number as we learned geometry. There are also questions contrived to lead the children on a journey of discovery and learning. What is your idea of the ideal classroom? or What is the biggest change that has happened in your town since you were born? are questions that inspired building our own desks and writing a book about the effects of the construction of a local bike path on our community.

My hope is that this book will be an encouragement to teachers. To some, the book may be a glimpse into a whole new way of thinking about education. Others may find their own ideas confirmed or be challenged to expand and deepen the practices they have already begun to employ. Still others may see the book as only a beginning and develop the ideas further in their own thinking and classrooms. My intention is to provide a philosophical framework and a variety of practical examples that will equip and inspire teachers to develop curriculum with their own children rather than replicate the projects described. There may be ideas throughout the book that will seem worth apprehending and I offer them freely, but I trust teachers will discern the foundation from which they spring and build their own designs upon it. I believe children long for authority born of their own teacher's creative imagination, which truly "authors" the learning activities of the class.

I hope the book will also be of value to people preparing to be teachers. Future educators need to develop strong ideals about and a practical understanding of students, teaching, and curriculum. They will benefit from seeing rich examples of what is possible for our students to achieve. I think it would be a valuable exercise for people entering the teaching profession to analyze the curriculum projects described in Chapters 3 through 9 in the light of the principles of inquiry and authentic teaching defined in Chapters 1 and 2. Where do the projects manifest the ideals, where do they fall short, how might they be improved?

I hope this book will also be of interest to parents. The methods of teaching and learning described here are as valuable for parents to apply in the home as they are for teachers in the classroom. The ideas and examples in this book will be especially useful to parents who are educating their children at home or who like to engage in learning projects and activities with their children.

Business members in the community will find suggestions for ways in which they might become involved in the schools. I hope they will be inspired by the examples of the effects their participation can have on student learning.

Finally, I hope the book will influence those who determine educational policy and curriculum frameworks on the local, state, and national level and anyone else who has an interest in how we can prepare our children to lead our nation into a new century.

CHAPTER ONE

Finding the Genius

I don't teach from a theory or a model. In fact, I am usually fairly unconscious about what I do on the front lines, guided by intuition and instinct. Only when I look back on my work do I begin to articulate the principles and ideals that guide me.

When I think back on a curriculum project, it seems like it all just happened. One thing led naturally to another. I gave the children a few challenges and developed the curriculum out of their responses. On the other hand, projects like this *don't* just happen. They grow out of very fundamental principles concerning children, teachers, and curriculum. So first I should unpack the assumptions about learning that guide my intuitions every moment of every school day.

Getting to the Point

I used to live across the street from the Arnold Arboretum in Jamaica Plain, Massachusetts, a glorious park where trees from all over the world mingled. This "United Nations" of trees was also the gathering place of every neighborhood dog that had escaped the leash. My daughter Mariam, who was a little over a year old at the time, loved to see the dogs when we went walking in the park. *Da* was her first word, and I'm still not sure if she meant *dad* or *dog*. Both were of equal importance to her.

One morning I looked out the window and saw a particularly

exuberant pack of dogs convening under the tall Norway pines. They were leaping and licking, sniffing and scratching. Calling Mariam to the window, I pointed across the street to the dogs. She looked up at my pointing finger with mild interest. "No, da!" I cried. "Over *there!* Across the street!" Realizing that *over* and *across*, like all prepositions, do not mean much to a one-year-old child, I pointed more vigorously to the cavorting canines. However, the more animatedly I pointed, the more interested Mariam became in my pointing finger. I could not get her to look at the dogs.

My teacher instincts recognized an important lesson here. Focusing on the pointer instead of the focal point is an almost universal tendency. For teachers, it points (forgive me) to our propensity to focus on methods rather than objectives, materials rather than processes, techniques rather than understanding, and organizational structures rather than vision. We look for the program that will motivate all students, the text that will meet the needs of all children, the procedures that will ensure discipline and order, and the policies and structures that will guarantee successful educational reform. We forget that all these "pointers" have their origin and intent in the goals and objectives of our endeavor. If we adopt the materials and methods without understanding their purpose, we are like Mariam looking at my finger. Perhaps that is why our pedagogy sways with the currents of the latest educational fads and innovations. If we try to serve the fruit without any knowledge of the root, we can deliver a tasty meal or two, but we will not be able to sustain growth. When the fruit is gone, we will look for a new tree.

Before we can make meaningful use of the many tools and structures designed to help educate our children, we need to develop a vision of what is important for our children to learn. As Tom James (1991), professor of education at Brown University, writes, "To start a school is to determine what it means to be a human being."

In the reality of the classroom, our effectiveness as teachers is not reflected in the materials and structures of our pedagogy as much as it is in the countless decisions we make every day, decisions that are made in an instant and that cannot be anticipated by even the best lesson plan. These decisions establish our character and authority as teachers and demonstrate our values to the children in our care. They spring from our deepest intuitions, our most basic beliefs of what it means to be a teacher, our vision of the kind of human beings we are striving to inspire. Do I help him with that problem or let him struggle? Do I pursue her question or stick with the lesson? Does this behavior need to be punished or ignored? Does this composition need to be criticized or praised? If we are not clear about the goal of our efforts, our judgments will not be guided by a consistent purpose and understanding. We will lack the discernment to determine how and when to use the methods and materials of our trade. We will either hold on tenaciously to the structures we know or fall prey to the latest fads. Although cooperative learning, thematic teaching, constructivism, whole language, all have much to offer students and teachers alike, if they do not inform our understanding of children and how they learn, of our roles as teachers, and of the curriculum we teach, then they are likely to be washed away by the next wave of reform that crashes on the banks of our classrooms.

Who are these children? What can I do as their teacher? What am I supposed to teach? Not until we come to grips with these essential questions will we begin to approach the object toward which all the structures and techniques point: preparing our children to manifest the fullness of their humanity in their thoughts, their feelings, and their deeds.

Who Are These Children?

Teachers often labor under the assumption that we need to meet the needs of *all* the children in our classes. We have children who are able to read Shakespeare and children who can barely read at all. We have children who can do algebra and children who cannot do simple addition. To compound these tremendous discrepancies, we are expected to teach our students in heterogeneous groups rather than separate them by ability. And if this weren't enough, with the advent of inclusion we have some children in our classes who can't see or hear and some who are confined to wheelchairs. We also have an increasing number of children who cannot speak English. I am all for inclusion, but working under these conditions, we barely hold on to the children with pressing academic needs, we throw an occasional bone to challenge the ones who are bored, and we do all we can to keep the children in the middle somewhat productive and involved. How can we meet the needs of all these children?

If we try to meet everyone's needs, I see no way to avoid going home at the end of the day in frustration. No matter how hard conscientious teachers work, we labor under a cloud of guilt because we know we are not doing the job. No matter what we do to teach our students what they need to know, we always seem to fall short. On Sunday nights our hearts beat with anxiety rather than enthusiasm for the week ahead.

I don't know about you, but I hate feeling guilty. I don't like the children in my class to take on tasks they cannot accomplish, and I don't like to either. I found I needed to set a new goal to guide my teaching, one that I had a reasonable chance of reaching. So I asked myself a new question: How can I create an environment that allows every child to express and develop his or her true genius, the essence of who he or she really is? In doing so I had shifted my entire focus: rather than trying to meet the needs of every single child, I concentrated on shaping the learning environment to enable each child to manifest the genius that he or she brought to the classroom.

I use the word *genius* intentionally. I do not mean to suggest that every child is a genius as we understand that word today, but rather that everyone *has* a genius according to the word's essential meaning of "a particular character or essential spirit." It is the quality that makes something unique. A place has a genius, so does a particular time. Teachers need to develop an eye to discern the genius of the American Revolution in history, the Pythagorean theorem in mathematics, or even the comma in writing mechanics. We especially need to recognize the genius in our students, that quality or collection of qualities that makes them who they are, that distinguishes them from everyone else. I want to celebrate the unique expression of humanity that each one represents. Even the ones who drive me crazy! I have discovered that when children know that I recognize who they are, they will open up in trust and present me with the fullness of their capability to learn. They will be accessible to what I have to teach them. Whatever ability they have in any given subject will be applied without reservation.

Children bring a wide variety of unique qualities into our class-rooms. Genius manifests in many areas other than the traditional intellectual functions with which it is usually identified. Howard Gardner (1983) opened the door to our understanding that there are many ways in which children can be smart. He identified seven intelligences: linguistic, logical-mathematical, spatial, musical, bod-ily-kinesthetic, interpersonal, and intrapersonal. On the basis of his continuing research, he is considering adding more. My guess is that if we observe correctly, we will see that each child has his or her own way of being smart.

Too often our classrooms are designed for the children who are at home in the abstractions of linguistic and logical-mathematical thinking, leaving many others to feel that school is not for them. Students who learn and express themselves in more concrete or imaginative ways struggle with the abstract thinking required and fall further and further behind. Eventually they lose hope and either distract the class or retract from it. Not only do these individual students suffer, but the class community loses the valuable contribu-tions they might make. For example, Yolanda, the peacemaker who cannot read but who understands the feelings and motivations of her classmates in a far subtler way than I, retreats from the class and no one can solve the constant fighting between Jeff and Raphael. Mark, the artist who cannot write, withdraws into his own world, and the pictorial expressions of his understanding are lost. Kyle, the organizer who struggles in math, finds no way to apply his gifts in school and begins running illicit operations on the streets. Many children with valuable skills like Jessica, Mark, and Kyle feel their genius is not recognized or valued in the traditional structures of our schools.

While I do not always recognize the genius in every child, I sometimes have an insight that penetrates beneath visible behavior and reveals who a certain child really is. When I do, I see a quite different child from the one who is constantly acting out in class.

No one liked Arthur much. Teachers whose classes he had been in warned me to watch out. They weren't fooling. Arthur knew the answer to everything. And he was not shy to tell you. He had a slightly affected British accent in the fourth grade. He had zero tolerance for anyone else's ideas or points of view. If I ever put him in a group with other children he would usually storm out after a few minutes. "Those steewpid kids," he would grumble, "they don't listen to me." It was easy to see why Arthur had few friends in class.

One day while I was watching him alienate his peers, it suddenly dawned on me who Arthur was. He was royalty! All he wanted was to assume his rightful place on the throne and tell people what to do. And here he was, stuck in the body of a nine-year-old. A prince in exile! I suddenly had compassion for him.

"Arthur," I apologized, "I am so sorry. I didn't know." I explained that I had discovered his secret, and told him he and I had to begin our leadership training right away. If he assumed the throne with the same attitude he had in class, no one would ever listen to him. He might even be assassinated. I told him the story of the executions of Charles I and Louis XVI. We discussed the qualities a good leader should have. He needed to have compassion and understanding. He needed to bring the best out of all his subjects. He needed to learn to listen to their hopes and concerns.

By the end of the year, Arthur was a different person. Just like in the fairy tale, the toads that used to come out of his mouth became gold coins. He was considerate of others. He had found his place in the class community.

Arthur's transformation demonstrates the tremendous power we have as teachers. We can enable our children to become what we see in them. His story also illustrates how important it is for us to delight in what we see. All good teachers will tell you that the most important quality they bring to their teaching is their love for the children.

But what does that really mean? It means that before we can teach them, we need to delight in them. Someone once said that children need one thing in order to succeed in life: someone who is crazy about them. We need to find a way to delight in all our students. We may be the only one in their lives to do so. We need to look for the best, expect the best, find something in each child that we can truly treasure. Seeing the genius of a child is the key. I had real trouble delighting in Arthur until I was able to see him in his royal light. I don't mean to suggest that Arthur was truly the descendent of a royal line, but I did see he had qualities of leadership that were not being channeled properly. The royalty image was a concrete way to show him I saw his inner gift and his inner struggle. As he learned to relate to other children in the class, he felt less of a need to put himself above them. My seeing the world through his eyes inspired compassion and delight in me and freed the princely genius in him.

Arthur's story is also exceptional because I don't usually get the kind of insight that revealed the secret of Arthur's discontent. Since I'm not always able to see the genius in every child and provide just what he or she needs, I do the next best thing: I take the pot-shot approach. I try to have as many kinds of activity as possible going on in my classroom. I fill it with music, art, poetry, drama, sports, and crafts, along with the usual academic subjects. I regard them all as equally important and involve all the children in all of them, often as a whole class. This way, I am usually able to find some area in which each child can excel, some activity in which each can shine.

Jenny had many difficulties in school. She couldn't read, and she couldn't do even the most basic math. There seemed to be nothing in school for her. I tried dancing, singing, poetry, but nothing awakened her confidence. She was good at knitting, but it brought her no real pleasure. It wasn't until the last week of school I found the activity that revealed her genius. We were creating watercolor paintings to cover books we were making. Jenny's pictures were extraordinary. Her sense of form and color was magnificent. I did not have to praise her paintings, as I had tried to do with her knitting and singing to no avail. Her accomplishment was intrinsically satisfying. The other children saw it immediately and crowded around her table, offering encouragement and praise. But it was the last week of school. Had I known earlier, I would have painted with the whole class every week!

I do not just let the children do whatever they want, working only in areas in which they are talented. In fact, I think the times I do them the most good are when I help them go against their grain, do work that does not come easily. When children are recognized for their strengths, they are more willing to expose their weaknesses. When they have been honored for their uncanny ability to juggle bean bags, they are more willing to try to juggle numbers in math. When they have been applauded for their genius in solving math problems, they are more willing to give their best shot on the basketball court.

If children recognize that we have seen their genius, who they really are, they will have the confidence and resilience to take risks in learning. I am convinced that many learning and social difficulties would disappear if we learned to see the genius in each child and then created a learning environment that encourages it to develop.

One year I wrote a letter to my prospective fourth graders asking them to collect a box of souvenirs to help recall the events of summer. They would each report on their collection as a way of getting to know each other in September.

Since I was teaching in Lexington, an affluent community outside Boston, I expected to hear about some spectacular summer adventures. I was not disappointed. One girl went white-water rafting in Wyoming. Another, horseback riding in Montana. One boy told about his trip to Australia. Another, about his journey in the jungles of Borneo. Several spent weeks at various sport camps, perfecting backstrokes, bunts, dribbles, and slap shots. I was especially envious of Jon and his father, who caught a 140-pound halibut off the shore of Homer, Alaska. Each report was delivered in some detail, clear and organized, accompanied by airline ticket stubs, souvenirs, and spectacular photographs.

But nothing in my four years of teaching in Lexington prepared me for Leroy's summer adventure. Leroy rides a school bus for forty-five minutes every morning from Mattapan, where he lives with his mother and grandfather in a three-room apartment in which he shares a room with his two sisters.

Leroy was excited when his turn came to share his summer adventures. He strode to the front of the room with long, undulating steps. He turned to face the class and presented his box, a shoe box. It was empty. Out of a big grin he spoke with pride and enthusiasm unmatched by his well-traveled classmates. "This summer my mom got me a new pair of sneakers." He went on to describe the deal his mom got from "Harry the Greek" and his excitement in taking the sneakers home.

"Stand up on the desk, Leroy, so we can all see."

He didn't hesitate. The sneakers were black with white trim, a brand I had never heard of. He towered above the class, almost within reach of the ceiling.

"I got them in the middle of the summer," he continued, "but my mom wouldn't let me wear them until the first day of school."

"Wasn't that hard?" someone asked.

"Yeah, that was hard, all right." And then in a whisper in case his mom might be listening over the intercom or something, "Sometimes at night I'd sneak over and take them out of the box." His dark eyes glowed with excitement. "I loved to open the lid and smell them." He gave a deep sniff. "And if my mom went to sleep before me, I would put them on and walk around in my room. But I had to be careful not to wake my sisters."

He spoke with more passion about those shoes than Jon had about his halibut or Peter had about strange bats in the jungles of Borneo. I believe at that moment anyone in the class would have traded his or her summer excursion for one secret night with Leroy's sneakers.

"Leroy, I bet you can really jump in those shoes," I challenged.

"Yeah, I sure can."

"Here, take this chalk and see how high a mark you can make on the door."

Leroy got down from the desk. He took the chalk from my hand, hesitating for a moment to see if I was serious. My eyes said, Hit the moon, Leroy! He walked over to the door, leapt up, and left a white streak higher than the doorjamb. The class cheered.

"A mighty jump, Leroy!" I cried.

"Yeah," he said with a knowing smile, "but tomorrow I will be able to jump a lot higher."

"Why is that?"

"Because it's my birthday" was his matter-of-fact reply.

"Why will you be able to jump higher on your birthday?"

"'Cause it's my birthday," he repeated, somewhat perturbed at my questioning something so obvious.

"You mean you think that tomorrow when you wake up you will be taller because it's your birthday?"

"Yeah, I will." I pressed him on the point. He was certain. I was amazed he could think this on the eve of his tenth birthday. But he was so sure of himself that I didn't try to convince him otherwise. I would let him find out for himself.

"All right, Leroy. We'll try again tomorrow and see if you can jump any higher."

"I will."

The next day was Leroy's birthday. I drew my own card, of a pair of sneakers being zapped by bolts of lightning, and put it on the door. The class came in.

"Hey, look Leroy!" they shouted, pointing to the card on the door.

"Cool," he beamed.

We began our morning work, and it wasn't until 11:00 that we had time for Leroy to make another jump.

"Ready, Leroy?"

"I'm ready."

"Are you bigger today?"

"Yeah, I am."

"Okay," I said, "let's see."

Again Leroy took the chalk from my hand, this time with no hesitation. He crouched down, wound himself up like a spring, and in a sudden burst shot up like a rocket. The white streak flashed above the door. Two inches higher than yesterday's jump! He looked at me confidently. It was no surprise to him. He had never doubted it.

Someday I would tell him about gradual growth and the difference between older and taller. But his bright confidence at that moment seemed more important than a biologically correct view of physical development. Leroy was ten years old that day, and in the eyes of everyone in Room 9, he was two inches taller.

Who Are These Teachers?

Just as every child has a genius, so does every teacher. Each one of us must teach out of his or her own genius. The curriculum in every classroom should be shaped by each teacher's unique gifts, training, and interests. Our natural *authority* in the classroom is based on our *author*ship of the activities and experiences we use to engage the children. Because each teacher needs to find his or her own way, there is no one right way to "do it."

Mrs. Boyd's and Mrs. Greene's genius is apparent in the organization of their classrooms and the thoughtfully planned activities they design. Every item in their rooms speaks of careful planning and intelligent order. Everything has its correct place. The children are absolutely clear about what is expected. In years of teaching next to them, I'm still waiting for some of it to rub off. But that is their genius, and their children prosper under it.

Mr. Clark's genius is in his humor. Ms. Thomas enlivens every subject with the knowledge gained on her own travels around the world. Mr. Francis used to be an architect and applies his experience in design to many aspects of the curriculum.

Nevertheless, even though we have unique gifts and interests, all teachers share a common responsibility.

The Role of Every Teacher

I am fascinated with the origin of words. I am not a linguist, but I have found that tracing the evolution of a word often provides insights into the meanings and nuances of its modern use. The word *education* comes from a Latin root, *educare*, meaning to rear, to bring up. Another Latin word closely related to *educare* and often used in the same sense is *educere*, which means to draw or bring out. Our modern word *educe* is derived from *educere*. I like the idea of education as eduction, a process by which we draw out and develop something that is already there. Too often we think our role as teachers is to fill up. The empty children come before us and it is our job to fill them up with knowledge and understanding. That view puts us in the position of acting as if we possess knowledge and dispense it to our students. This kind of learning environment not only bores the children but also robs them of the opportunity to discover meaning and build understanding for themselves. The excitement and joy of learning for the student is in the chase, the discovery. For the teacher, it is in bringing out the experiences that will shed light on the path and illuminate the treasure.

When we focus too much on providing the answers, we neglect to perform in our most important teacher role: as an example of a learner. That is, after all, most fundamentally what we are trying to teach our students: how to learn. My favorite projects have been the ones I started out knowing the least about. In fact, I find it an interesting paradox that when I know a lot about the subject, the children tend to sit back expecting me to deliver the information to them out of my vast bank of knowledge. Neil Postman (1995) suggests that one of the most direct ways to improve education in our schools would be to require teachers to teach subjects they do not usually teach. The math teacher would teach art and the art teacher would teach science and the science teacher would teach English. Teaching subjects in which we are not naturally gifted, which may even be difficult for us, will put us in the right mind to understand how difficult learning can be for the children.

Not that there is anything wrong with having knowledge about a subject we are teaching. The more a teacher knows about a subject, the more likely he or she will be able to discern its genius. But if we really want to engage our children, we need to bridle our propensity to pontificate. The less I know about a subject, the easier that is to do. The children sense my curiosity and are eager to join in. They become active in pursuing knowledge, and I get excited by the process of learning along with them. I show them how to identify resources, what to do when we come to problems, and how to persevere when the going gets tough.

A teacher who draws out rather than fills up starts with the innumerable experiences the children have already had and then finds ways to connect these experiences to the concepts or principles in the curriculum. This might be called teaching by analogy or metaphor. We take something known and compare it to something unknown. One good example was a lesson on the absolute monarchy of Louis XIV. I told the class how as a child Louis was required to practice handwriting by copying over and over the following phrases: "Homage is due to kings. Their will is law. Kings can do no wrong. They do as they please." I wanted the class to understand what it was like to live under the rule of absolute power such as Louis held over the French people.

What experience did the children have that I could draw out and connect to the concept of absolute power? The closest one I could think of was the game Four Square. The way my students play it, whoever gets into the fourth square can make up the rules. That person's will is law. He can do no wrong. She does as she pleases, and the others in the class have no choice but to obey. When a student attains the fourth square, he or she feels what it is like to rule the kingdom. Students in the other three squares identify with the help-lessness and frustrations of the French people. Because of their own experience of being arbitrarily controlled by one person, they under-stand why the people were incited to rebel against their king.

This game can also be used to help them understand the confu-sion that followed the French Revolution. If the other players refuse to obey the rules decreed by the king in the fourth square, the king has little power. But neither does anyone else, so there will be much dispute about which rules to follow. Therefore, in Four Square, just as in constitutional government, everyone needs to agree to an objective set of rules no matter who is in power if the game is actually to be played instead of fought.

Experience is not a substitute for knowledge. I am not suggesting that we teach the French Revolution during recess. Experience sets the table for reflection. We still need to read, study, analyze, and compare the personalities and events that shaped this important historical era. But when the children can experience the feelings of the people as well as learn the facts, their knowledge will be warmed by their passions. When they can view a historical event through the lens of their own experience, all children will have a way to understand it. As Ralph Waldo Emerson ([1841] 1946) writes, "The child interprets the age of chivalry by going through his own age of chivalry, the age of maritime adventure by going through quite similar miniature experiences of his own. To the sacred history of the world he has the same key."

Before I tell my students about Magellan, I have to get them in touch with the first time they ventured into an unknown place. For one child it is entering the woods behind his backyard; for another, crossing the street by himself for the first time; and for a third, walking alone in the dark labyrinth of her father's warehouse. After we have discussed their experiences, I tell them about Magellan, and we learn about other explorers who knew similar fears in places none of their countrymen had ever ventured. The children have the feeling, Yeah, I'm one of those. I'm in that club. They feel like they are studying earlier club members rather than some remote, irrelevant historical persons.

If we can't find a correspondence to the curriculum in the children's experience, we first have to create the experience. King Arthur's teacher, Merlin, was a master at this. He changed Arthur into various animals to teach certain lessons. When Merlin wanted to show what a society was like in which the individual was totally subjugated to the needs of the society, he turned Arthur into an ant and sent him to live in an ant community.

I was teaching a fourth-grade class in 1992, and wanted to help my children understand the extraordinary events in Europe and the Soviet Union as the Communist world fell. Lacking the transforming powers of Merlin, I needed to find another way to help my children understand communism and the dismantling of the Berlin Wall. I found a unique opportunity for them to experience the contrast between socialism and capitalism when, as part of the project I describe in Chapter 3, we began the year in an empty classroom.

The first thing the students wanted in their room was pencils. I asked them how they wanted to store their pencils, because there wasn't anywhere to put them. "Shall we keep them all in a box and take them out when we need them? Or shall each person keep his or her own?" After some discussion, the children decided to own the pencils collectively. I think sharing sounded to them like the higher moral ground. We put the pencils in a box and everyone was free to take one out when needed but was expected to put it back when finished. It wasn't long before the last one to the box found no pencils. It wasn't much longer before the last five found no pencils. Students began holding on to the pencils rather than putting them back. As good as the idea of sharing the pencils sounded, it did not work. The idea of collective ownership did not correspond to the realities of human nature.

We then experimented with private ownership. Each one took care of his or her own pencil. Writing activities went smoothly until one afternoon an argument broke out.

"Hey, that's my pencil."

"No way! It's definitely mine."

They tried identifying their pencils with some distinguishing mark to avoid disputes, but problems persisted. Private ownership had limitations as well. We had experienced in a very local way the dilemma between collective and private ownership.

We were studying the Pilgrims at the time, so we did some research to find out how they resolved the question of ownership. We read in William Bradford's diary that in the early years of the Plimoth Plantation, everything was owned collectively. The land and houses all belonged to the community. The food grown by the men went into the common store, the clothes sewn by the women went into the common store, and people took out food and clothing according to their need.

A few years later Bradford wrote that the community was in a terrible crisis. They did not have enough food. Morale was low. A town meeting was held at which it was decided to give each family their own property. They could keep whatever they produced. In a very short time, food production dramatically increased. Women, who until this time never worked on the farm, joined their husbands in the fields, bringing their children with them. The incentive of being able to keep what was produced was extremely effective in inspiring the people to work hard. In the first few years of the European settlement in this country, the settlers experienced the transition from socialism to capitalism.

Capitalism creates a whole new set of problems, of course. What about poor widows or sick people who can't work? They would be taken care of in a socialist system. Must they starve in a private economy? I asked the children what they thought the Pilgrims should have done. They suggested a certain portion of whatever was produced be taken from each family and put into the common store to be used to help those in need.

"Does that remind you of something today?" I asked.

"Taxes!" cried Lilly.

Sure enough, we work and get money for our labor, but we each give a portion of our earnings to the "common store" to meet our joint concerns and to help those who are in need.

My students' own experience with the pencils and their research about the Pilgrims gave them a measure of understanding of complex world events. They were able to engage in meaningful discussions about socialism, capitalism, and taxes.

The principle of finding the genius, drawing it out, and connecting it to the world guides us in the development of curriculum and also in our everyday discussions in class. I try not to tell the children correct answers in our discussions, but instead to draw the answer out of them. I ask questions, listen to their responses, and show them how to test the validity of their hypotheses. I was recently teaching a third-grade class in Dubuque, Iowa. I told the children that when

I left Boston the temperature was forty degrees. But in my town of Lexington, about ten miles northwest of Boston, the temperature was only thirty degrees. I asked the children what might account for the difference. One child said maybe it was because Boston was closer to the equator. What a great hypothesis! Instead of just telling her no, I asked the class to look at a map. Sure enough, Boston was slightly closer to the equator. To help her discover that the distance from the equator wasn't the primary factor, I had her and another girl stand at the back of the room. I told one of them to take one step toward me. (With more time we could have measured the distance to scale.) Could the girl who was one step closer to me hear me better than the girl who was a step behind? We tried a few experiments, and anything one girl heard, the other did also. In the same way, I explained, being closer to the equator than Lexington was did not make Boston warmer. I never said no to the wrong answer. I just restated the hypothesis and helped the class explore it and discover for themselves whether it was correct. In this particular instance, because we could not examine the girl's equatorial hypothesis directly, I introduced a "metaphoric" example.

The point is to keep the idea alive by guiding them to consider it in a form they can tangibly experience. When they discover the answer for themselves, they understand it, remember it, and apply it to real situations. They participate in the process of thinking: they start with an observation and develop it through questioning, hypothesizing, analyzing, and testing until they can draw an accurate conclusion—a process I repeat over and over until my students internalize it as a habit.

CHAPTER TWO

What Do We Teach?

After recognizing the genius in every child and creating a learning environment that draws it out, a teacher needs to decide what to teach. Although curriculum content might be determined by state or local frameworks, we can often choose the materials and methods of instruction. If our choices about what to teach are not based on our ultimate goals, the materials and methods we adopt become goals in themselves. Our objective will be to get through the book or to complete the steps of the method. In order to set the materials and methods in the *service* of our primary educational goals rather than let them direct those goals, we must wrestle with this question: What is important to teach and how will my children best learn it?

Too often we are limited by our own unconscious assumptions or ruled by those we inherit from the collective traditions of the past. The prevailing conception of curriculum operating in many schools today actually prevents rather than assists teachers in preparing our children with the habits and skills of mind, heart, and work that will enable them to be caring and responsible adults, productive workers, independent learners, and thoughtful citizens.

Obstructions to Dynamic Curriculum

I see four distinct ways in which our perceptions about what we are supposed to teach obstruct the dynamic excitement of learning that attracted us to this profession in the first place. These inhibitors are (1) the fragmentation of subject matter, (2) the abstraction of knowledge, (3) our reliance on prepared textbooks and learning kits, and (4) the expectation that we will cover vast areas of content.

Fragmentation

In most of our schools today, we divide learning into separate subjects. In order to define and focus on specific areas of content and types of skills, we teach our subjects in short blocks, neatly dividing the school day into periods of math, science, reading, and social studies. If our children are fortunate, they have additional blocks for art and music.

The education industry—book publishers, curriculum developers, consultants, specialists—produces an endless supply of textbooks, teaching materials, learning kits, and lesson plans that define subject content. They organize information, package it for presentation and provide practice drills and tests to determine if the children "get it." Math is taught in the math book, science in the science book, and social studies in the social studies book. Every subject is broken down into subcategories of facts and skills, bits of learning. The entire world, it seems, has been rigorously processed and packaged for student consumption.

Organizing learning in this way may be an effective means of teaching disassociated facts, but does it help our students understand the world? Does it prepare them to enter it as adults who have a passion for learning, who can create meaning from their observations and experiences? Will teaching unrelated facts inspire our children to seek meaning throughout their lives? Will they learn how to solve problems or how to work with others?

Compartmentalized learning does not help children reach our highest educational goals because it does not correspond to the way human beings experience life. It defines a world once removed from the way we actually interact with it. Presenting the world broken up into subjects puts it into a form already abstracted and shaped—predigested, if you will. It's like giving the children a coloring book or a paint-by-number set rather than a blank piece of paper, many means of filling it, and inspired guidance. It shows the children things it would be better to help them discover for themselves. It robs them of the opportunity to construct for themselves categories that give their observations personal relevance and meaning.

How do we learn naturally about the world? In reality, we experience the world whole, not broken into discrete chunks. We do not have mathematical experiences, scientific experiences, artistic experiences; we have experiences. It is in reflection, when we look back at our experiences and try to understand and communicate them, that we see them from the different points of view that correspond to the subjects we teach in school.

How Do We Help Students Discover the Origins of the Disciplines for Themselves?   Sid Smith, the director of the Authentic Teaching, Learning, and Assessment for All Students (ATLAS) project, suggests I put on my wall the most vital, essential questions I want each of my students to ask in the course of every learning project. We always ask the questions, but I've resisted putting anything on my wall, because I don't want my students to resort to a formulaic approach to learning. If I had to post guiding questions, however, they would be ones that help the children reflect on their experiences through the lenses of the disciplines:

1. *What is there to count and measure?* This is the authentic origin of mathematics. It leads us to explore our experience in terms of what numbers can reveal about reality.
2. *What are the variables?* This question launches scientific or historical investigation. What happens if I change certain variables? How will that affect the results? Can I predict what will happen?
3. *Have others ever had this experience, and what did they say about it?* This question opens the door to reading, which brings us in touch with the thoughts of those who have gone before us, charting the way and establishing the content and methods of inquiry in the specific disciplines.
4. *What do I want to communicate to others about my experience?* Serious learners have a responsibility to share what they learn

with others. Making ourselves clearly understood is the basis of effective communication: oral, written, visual, and dramatic.

5. *How does this experience resemble other experiences I have had?* This question prompts us to look across the disciplines, to discover relationships and connections with other experiences in our lives. This is the process by which meaning is defined and understanding cultivated.

6. *What does this experience teach me about myself, my responsibility, and my place in the world?* This is the culmination of all the other questions. Everything we learn in any subject should reveal something about who we are and our place in the world. This is the heart of social studies.

What Might This Process Look Like in the Classroom?   Suppose we leave a jar of water on the windowsill and watch it disappear over the next few days. That is our experience. That is what we observe with our senses.

First, I must hold back the conceptual thinkers from naming it (Oh, that's just evaporation) and racing on to the next question. Now, as we try to understand this phenomenon, reflecting on our experience in an effort to make sense and meaning of it, we open the doors to the different disciplines.

We need to make some measurements to calculate how much water disappears over a given time. At what rate is the water leaving the jar? This is the natural way our experience leads us into mathematics.

Next we begin to wonder what variables affect the disappearing water. Does it vanish at a different rate when we put it by the window? by the plants? in the closet? As we wonder about the variables and design experiments to determine which ones are significant, we enter the world of science.

Then we wonder if anyone else has ever had this experience, and if so, what she or he had to say about it. We read and do research to find out what the "experts" report. We explore the work of scientists who have labored to understand the mysteries of this phenomenon— and who have given it a name, *evaporation.* We conduct our own experiments and record our results for others to read. We practice our writing skills in reporting our observations. We draw diagrams when a picture can communicate more clearly than words. We try to represent the concept artistically, impersonating evaporation dramatically or representing its subtle movement in a watercolor painting. (Making a picture of a concept is a habit I have the children practice whenever possible.)

One child relates the experience to another he has had. The disappearing water reminds him of trying to see the clock's minute hand move. He knows it does, but is frustrated that he can never see it. He feels the same way about the water. He writes a poem relating the disappearing water to the passing of time.

Finally, we take a look at evaporation in our own bodies, and see how it parallels and differs from what we saw in the jar. Perhaps we investigate evaporation as a metaphor and discuss other phenomena to which it corresponds.

This is the progression for genuine learning that most closely matches our natural activity in the world. It begins with an experience, and then in reflection on that experience we lead the children to a meaningful involvement with the skills and content standards of the traditional subject areas. By discovering the origin of the disciplines themselves, children acquire a deeper understanding of their uniqueness and interconnectedness.

Abstractions

The separate subjects we abstract and present in standard forty-five-minute periods seem more natural to adults than to children because we have built up a large bank of concepts from years of experience and reflection. Our students' ability to conceptualize, however, is only beginning to develop. Their capacity to grasp abstract concepts is rudimentary, their experience is limited, and they have not developed the habit of reflection. They think in mental pictures rather than abstract concepts. If small children hear *mountain* they have an image of a mountain. But if they hear *subtraction*, *courage*, or *experiment* they are likely to be confused, even if they seem to understand.

However, children have, in fact, experienced what these abstract concepts "point to." They experience subtraction when they lose a mitten and notice that only one remains. They experience the courage of riding a two-wheeler or of turning a bedroom light off at night. In trying different ways to get something to work, they experience experimentation.

Children know first through the senses. They see, hear, touch, taste, and smell the world around them long before they can convert their experience into concepts. Concepts begin to become meaningful when they are connected directly to the experience. Children understand *hot* when the word is integrated with the experience of burning a finger. The concept of *fraction* becomes meaningful when they see a pizza cut in slices. We help our students build understanding by drawing out their experiences and connecting them to the concepts that lift them into consciousness and give them meaning.

Children also learn directly about the world and about themselves through feelings. Emotions are awakened as they interact with the world and with other people. If a child sees a candy bar, she may feel desire. If he hears thunder, he may feel afraid. If another child shares a snack with her, she may feel gratitude. Stories are a powerful way to inspire feelings. Love of goodness and truth, hatred of evil, respect for honesty, awe for the sublime, are all feelings that arise from hearing or reading stories.

Feelings reveal a different aspect of the world than our senses, but I call them both direct experiences because they happen naturally. We do not need to be educated to see, hear, touch. We do not need education to feel sad when Hansel and Gretel get lost in the woods, mad when the witch captures them, or happy when they are reunited with their father. We do need education to develop the abstract concepts to communicate our experience and understand it.

The natural and direct experience of interacting with the world, whether through our senses or our feelings, provides the foundation from which the concepts will grow. The concept is the culmination of the experience, like the flower that grows out of the roots, stem, and leaves. When a concept emerges from experience, thinking it becomes as powerful an experience as one directly sensual or emotional. That is when we say, Aha!

Unfortunately, we do not always take the time to help our children construct their own concepts from their experience. If we feed them abstract concepts without leading them through the prerequisite sensual and emotional experiences, the children who think visually just don't get it. The students more advanced in the ability to conceptualize learn to use the words, and seem to understand; but when they are pressed to explain or asked to apply their knowledge to a practical problem, the superficiality of their understanding is revealed. These students are quick to get the "name," to identify the concept, but they close the door to any further reflection. They don't ponder, wonder, ask questions, look deeper, make connections, have insights, or develop new ideas. They pick the flower off the stem, and though initially beautiful, it soon pales and withers. Such is the fate of concepts we disassociate from authentic encounters.

I am often surprised when I realize my students do not understand something I assumed they would. Even concepts that seem quite concrete can be several steps removed from the authentic experience the children need to build their own understanding. We need to train ourselves to see the hidden abstractions that are likely to cause confusion. For example, the letters of our alphabet used to be pictures of the world around us. But over time the pictures have been reduced to symbols that no longer resemble anything we can observe with our senses. They have become pure abstractions.

Sonya was a very mature first grader whose mother was concerned that she would be bored in my class because she already knew how to do everything in the first-grade curriculum. Mom was not pleased that I would be teaching a lesson on the letter M, when her daughter already knew how to read at the third-grade level. I taught it anyway, using a method we practiced at the Waldorf School. I told a story about the mighty, magic mountains. The children painted the mountains, and then discovered the M in the mountains they painted. They saw the V in the valley. The little girl said with no slight condescension, "Mr. Levy, I already knew how to make an M," then continued with delight and satisfaction at having made a great discovery, "but now I know what an M is!"

———————————— ❧ ————————————

When we teach the symbol without showing the child how it evolved from the concrete experience, we run the risk that he will get the name but not the concept, the form but not the understanding, the information but not the Aha!

Kits and Textbooks

The third problem with the curriculum is that teachers are conditioned to rely on the textbook or learning kit as the source of knowledge. Except for a required math text, I have never used a textbook or kit as the primary resource in my teaching. Actually, I did use a kit once. In my first year of teaching in Lexington, I was supposed to teach a fourth-grade class about rocks and minerals. I thought it would be important to have some good specimens on hand to show the children. I asked the science department if they had anything available. They sent me a kit. When I opened the box I was dismayed. There were loose rocks all over the place. Empty bags with labels like *obsidian, hematite, shale*. There were jars of vinegar, loose tiles, pieces of glass, and some steel nails. And of course, the teacher's manual. What am I going to do with this mess? I wondered. There is no way I can use this. Then it dawned on me: this was the *perfect* kit! I would put the mess before the children and challenge them to put the kit in order. They would have to learn the techniques for finding out what all the loose rocks were, and then put them in the proper bags. The difference between using the kit to teach the skills and learning the skills to put the kit in order is significant—it is at the heart of what distinguishes authentic teaching, learning, and assessment from the kind of activity, or lack of it, that characterizes much of what happens in our classrooms today. It is the difference between learning facts and skills and the Aha! that comes when we see how they are connected to real life. Putting the kit back together was a meaningful and authentic challenge rather than a prescribed set of activities designed to teach specific skills and facts. But those same skills and facts had to be learned in order to complete the task.

If we want teaching and learning to be truly authentic, we need to escape our reliance on prepackaged learning kits and textbooks as the source and focus of our curriculum. They may be useful resources in providing materials to work with or information for research, but they will not teach our children the skills and habits they need to reach our highest educational goals.

I always tell my students about Galileo. When he was in school his teachers told him emphatically that everything there was to know was known. If you wanted to find out what was true, you needed only to look in the books of Aristotle. That is where all truth and knowledge lived. His teachers taught everything by demonstration, never allowing the pupils to try something for themselves. "How do you know what you are saying is true?" Galileo would ask.

"Because it says so in the books of Aristotle." (No Aha! there.)

"But what if Aristotle was wrong?" Galileo would feel compelled to ask. He was expelled from school for his constant questioning.

I wonder what happens to the Galileos in our classrooms today. Does it seem to them that teachers think knowledge and truth—in short, the world—is found in kits and textbooks? That we learn about the world by filling in worksheets? What do we do for the children who want to get their own hands on the truth, discover what the world is about for themselves? Isn't that yearning to discover for oneself a quality we hope to cultivate in all our students?

But if we don't organize our lessons around prepared materials, where will they come from? Our challenge is to teach our children how to learn from the direct observations and experiences they have as they live their lives. Curriculum is most authentic when it arises out of the natural activity of people coming together. When people come together, they observe, question, compare experiences. This is the raw stuff from which learning begins.

I am always listening for a question or observation a child makes in class that might lead to a complex investigation of a topic relevant to the children and to the required curriculum. When we start from what the children bring, they get to see how thoughts and questions can arise from simple observations. They learn to explore the questions, deepen them, broaden them, and then design a plan to pursue the answer. One of the most important things we do is give our children the confidence that there is a way to find the answers to the questions they have. We show them how to track down the resources, how to collect data, how to experiment. In short, we teach them the methods of inquiry employed by the scientist or historian. We teach them the responsibility of communicating what they find to the community. We show them how to interact with the world in a thoughtful way.

"Covering" the Curriculum

A major gap exists between covering a subject and understanding it. Coverage generally implies an overview of facts. The children are responsible for learning the content and are tested to see how much they remember. My social studies curriculum goes from Magellan to the American Revolution. Many high school teachers are asked to teach from Magellan to the present time, all in one year! My math curriculum is teeming with new concepts and methods, in twelve dimensions. In order to get through all the material, we can't go into a single issue too deeply, can't look at information from multiple perspectives, can't allow the children to ask their own questions and construct their own knowledge. There isn't time to develop the habits and skills so important in creating thoughtful and responsible independent thinkers and learners.

As if the traditional subjects were not enough, every time some new need is perceived, we are asked to include it in our curriculum. Conflict management, social competency, self-esteem, drugs and alcohol, sexually transmitted diseases, all have worked their way into the curriculum, starting in the earliest grades in many schools. And with all that is added, nothing is ever taken away! Teachers responsible for covering all the content have no time to attend to students' questions, to lay a rich foundation, to orchestrate experiences that will enhance understanding, to give children multiple and rigorous challenges to demonstrate what they have learned.

Curriculum is more than the content of the subjects we teach. One of its goals is certainly the mastery of a specific body of knowledge. But beyond that, the subjects we focus on are *means* to teach our students how to observe, how to question, how to reason, how to analyze, how to plan, how to make decisions, how to communicate, and how to think. We also use subject content to awaken a desire for truth, a passion for understanding, a sense of the joy intrinsic in learning, and empathy for others. We use the curriculum to teach how to work with precision and care, to persevere, and to set high standards of achievement. The tension between covering content on the one hand and developing habits of mind, heart, and work on the other is at the heart of the debate in schools about what is important to teach.

Obviously, we want our children to master the content *and* develop the habits of mind, heart, and work. Our charge is to do it all. This burden produces a new cloak of guilt, a guilt I have not found a way to escape on my own. We cannot teach the breadth of the entire world and at the same time achieve any depth of understanding. Teachers are forced to choose among exhaustion, frustration, and superficiality.

Who Decides Curriculum?

In most schools, the district or the state provides the framework of required studies. The subjects we are to teach, the skills we are to develop, and the content we are to master is outlined to a lesser or greater degree. How can authentic projects arise from the learning community when the curriculum is dictated from above? On the other hand, if we teach what we want to or allow projects to emerge from the children's interests, how can the district ensure that the children will be exposed to a thorough and comprehensive program across the grades?

I do think we need some curriculum guidance from the central administration. We need to have a framework so that in the course of the children's education they will be exposed to an integrated and coherent course of study. We also need to coordinate the subjects across the grades so that the children do not learn about electricity three years in a row. We need an outline of when the children are expected to master sentence structure, fractions, scientific procedure. What I want from my system is a very broad sketch of subjects to teach and the freedom to teach them out of my own design. Tell me the children should learn about China, the Civil War, botany, or New England geography. Define the habits of mind, heart, and work that the community decides are important for all children to develop. Then let me have room to explore the topic with the children. I don't think it is necessary that every teacher teach in the same way or that every child have the same experience. If you told twenty artists to paint a river scene, you would get twenty very different renditions. In the same way, if you told twenty teachers to teach about rivers, you would get twenty different lessons. An exhibition of the river paintings in a gallery is enhanced by their similarities and differences. Likewise, the different experiences the children receive from year to year enhance rather than diminish discussions and activities that build on their understanding of rivers.

I want to teach out of the natural activity of the class. I want the children to see how learning is the natural activity of people coming together. I want to begin with the students' experience and their own questions. I want them to follow their own interests. But I also need to address the content and skills prescribed in the curriculum. Herein lies the art of teaching: leading the students from their own experiences and interests to the depth and breadth of the world within the framework of the subjects I am supposed to teach. I need to find the link that leads the children from their own interests and questions to the areas of the required curriculum.

Planning Curriculum

My colleague Sid Smith often presses me to define my process for designing curriculum and for connecting student interest to content. I tell him it is impossible, there is no formula. It happens in a different way every time. It is a complicated morass of thinking about ideas, activities, assessments, certainly as much a matter of insight and intuition as it is of strategy and planning. I decide more as we go along than I have planned in the beginning. But Sid's rigorous questions have helped me untangle the process, making it more clear to me and I hope more accessible to others.

The elements are these:

1. *Topic*. This is a subject required by the curriculum, such as simple machines, plants, or colonial life. It is important for me to have a good understanding of the content. The more I understand the subject, the more ways I will be able to relate it to students' lives. I know this seems to contradict what I said earlier about my favorite projects being the ones I know least about. Nevertheless, both statements are true.

2. *Genius of the topic*. This is the most important part of the process. I try to find the genius of the topic, what makes it unique. What is essential about the American Revolution? What is unique about the world of plants, what distinguishes them from all other forms of life? What is the genius of grammar? Finding the genius guides me in sorting through the pile of available information. It gives meaning and purpose to even the most mundane skills. (For example, what is the genius of spelling? For a long time, there was no such thing as correct spelling. We can thank—or blame—Noah Webster for establishing the first code of proper spelling in this country. But what was it really? A social convention. Spelling is not a right or wrong thing, like math, it is just an agreement to do it a certain way. You learn spelling as a courtesy to others. The genius of spelling is in courtesy, in its social contract.) Discerning the genius steers me in designing activities for the children to conduct. It also helps me decide which of the questions and ideas that the children bring in the course of the activities will lead us closer to the heart and which will be unfruitful tangents. Finding the genius of the topic is like setting the compass to true north. (It may be that as we study a topic the genius will unfold as something other than I had imagined. The class may find a different genius than I had seen. That is fine as long as they can support their claim with good methods of research or experimentation.)

3. *Illustrations*. I need to find the best examples of the expression of this genius. In history, I look for it in biographies of persons who embody in their lives the struggles of an age. A biography makes the abstract elements of cause and effect concrete. It sets the principles I want to teach in the context of a story. In science, I try to find the manifestation of the concept in the natural world. For a mathematical concept, like telling time, I might try to discover its origin: What do you think was the first time anyone needed to know what time it was? These real-life illustrations provide the ore from which the children will mine the genius.

4. *Experiences:* I need to find examples in the children's experiences that parallel (on a small scale) the principles I am trying to teach them about the world. This is the bridge that connects their experience to the content of the required curriculum. I ask myself: What experiences have the children had that are miniature examples of the principle or concept I want them to understand? For example, if I want second graders to understand the concept of *metamorphosis*, what in their lives is a direct experience of it, even though they may have never heard the term? Maybe they have seen a caterpillar spin a chrysalis and emerge as a butterfly. If they have not had any such experiences, I have to create them in the class before I can teach the concept.

5. *Questions*. I need to think of questions that will draw out the students' experiences and other questions that will help them see connections between their experiences and the same principles as they manifest in the world. If you were to disappear today, how might I find out something about your life? prompts children to think of the kind of records and artifacts that are evidence of their existence. Then I might ask, How do we know anything today about Paul Revere? Having reflected on their own artifacts helps them understand the methods of the historian in interpreting the past.

6. *Story*. Children pay attention to a story. I have to figure out a way to put the content I want them to master into a story.

There needs to be a progression with a beginning, middle, and end. There needs to be the dramatic tension between protagonist and antagonist. A story keeps all the children involved and motivated. It facilitates memory and increases understanding. For example, what is the story of a plant? The stages of development offer a context for beginning, middle, and end. The plant starts as a compact seed; expands into roots, stems, and leaves; contracts again into buds; expands again in the blossom; and contracts again in the fruit and seed. And the whole process goes on "happily forever after" as the seeds fall to the ground and the stages start anew. There might be a story in the sacrifice of the lower leaves, which die off as the plant sends the most refined juices to nourish the production of the fruit. Or in the sacrifice of producing a fruit at all! What good is the green pepper for the plant? If a plant was interested just in survival and propagation, would it design a green pepper? or a watermelon? Why should the apple tree put so much of its resources into producing apples, which do very little for the tree? Yes, its tastiness attracts birds to eat the seeds and spread them afar, and I suppose there is some nourishment that comes to the soil as the flesh decomposes. But the apple seems an extravagant product for those functions. The production of food gets to the genius of the plant. A plant doesn't need to go to the store to buy food; it can make its own! Does it make a little extra for you and me? The plant has many antagonists, so there are many other good stories of how it defends itself from the cold, the heat, drought, shade, overcrowding. Perhaps its most interesting enemy is gravity, which it works against as it pushes upward toward the sun with the power of life.

7. *Activities*. The activities often arise out of the experiences I design for the children so that they will have a direct and personal link to the concepts. I try to think of activities that are open-ended enough to allow for a wide range of participation, depending on the children's developmental stage and ability. The activities often follow the basic curriculum framework of designing questions, researching answers, collecting

and analyzing data, and sharing what is learned with the community. But sometimes the activity is the point of departure in the planning process. I may have an idea to do an archaeological dig. Then I think of ways to connect the activities and skills needed in excavating a site to my required curriculum.

8. *Skills and habits*. I have to be clear what skills and habits I want to teach. For example, my children need to learn how to use capital letters, so I make sure to include reading activities in which they can discover the patterns of capitalization and writing activities in which they can practice using capital letters. I also want them to develop the habit of distinguishing between facts and assumptions, so I find repeated opportunities for them to practice telling the difference.

9. *Evaluation*. Throughout a project I informally evaluate students' participation in our class discussions and the clarity with which they can express their ideas in speech, in writing, and through artistic activity. I evaluate their methods of research, including data collection and analysis, interviewing skills, questioning ability, and variety of resources. I make sure each one is doing more than he or she thought possible. Of primary importance is their demonstration that they understand the genius of our subject, for that is also a measure of how effective my teaching is. Writing assignments, experiment records, historical studies, and math projects are developed through several drafts and finally put on a high-quality "book paper" (they get just one piece for each assignment; any mistakes must be creatively incorporated into the design of the page). Many of these projects are written and illustrated with great care. At the end of the year we bind these pages together into a book that serves as a record of all they learned during the year.

Although I've numbered these elements 1 through 9, implying a sequence, I can start with any of them. Maybe as I stumble over a shovel on my way to the pencil sharpener, I get an idea to build a shed to store our tools. Then I think of ways to connect this to our required curriculum: measurement in mathematics; simple machines in science; building shelter in social studies; communicating our progress in language arts.

My thought process might go something like this: What's the genius of a toolshed? Is it in the importance of taking care of things? What does that mean, to take care of things? Where else will that concept be applicable? Can I find stories in which failing to care for tools interferes with an important mission? Can I make one up if I can't find one already written? Did it ever happen in our class? What is it about building things, anyway? Where did that idea begin? Do the children have things worth protecting? Have they ever built something to protect their stuff? Protect from what? Who is the enemy? Why don't we just leave our tools outside? After such pondering I would think of ways to involve the community, because I don't know a thing about building sheds!

Or I may begin with a topic we are required to study. We teach the discovery of the New World in fourth-grade social studies. What is the genius of the Age of Exploration? What motivated it? Where is the story in it? What was gained? What was lost? How have the children experienced exploration in their own lives? What questions can I ask to draw their experiences out? What can we do to demonstrate what we learn?

Or maybe there is a certain habit I want the children to develop. How can I build a sense of gratitude in my students? What can I do to teach them the process of designing and writing up a scientific experiment, or evaluating news reports or historical analysis for bias? Whatever the entry point for designing curriculum, I will consider all nine elements in the course of its implementation.

Elements of Authentic Curriculum

I look for certain qualities in evaluating the potential and effectiveness of a curriculum project. First, it should originate from the natural activity of the learning community. I like to support the idea that knowledge is not limited to books and kits. I want the children to see that it arises as naturally as breathing when people come together to observe the world around them and share experiences. The best projects are those that arise spontaneously out of a class discussion or activity. The next best are those that seem as if they do.

Second, an authentic curriculum project is original. Students are motivated when they feel the excitement of embarking on a journey that has never been taken before. They feel like pioneers or explorers. If they see signs along the way that others have been here, they are curious to see what record they left. They experience the joy and thrill of learning. Each year I try to do at least one major project that has not been done before.

Third, good projects engage all the disciplines and multiple intelligences. They provide an opportunity to develop basic skills in the context of meaningful and purposeful activities. Different components of the project involve and challenge the children academically, socially, physically, artistically, musically, and technologically. I want to give all the children the opportunity to express their particular gift and develop areas of weakness.

Fourth, I like the projects to lead to primary resources. Research should lead to original texts and artifacts. If we collect our own data, it should be unique, relevant, and significant.

Fifth, it is important to involve the community. Community members have a variety of expertise to offer to the children, and the children need to feel the security and responsibility of being part of their community.

Finally, the results of an authentic project have meaning. They are of interest to other people in and outside the school. The products the children produce to share what they have learned must be interesting to the community at large. When the children feel the community is interested in what they are doing, they will be motivated to do their best work and strive to achieve the highest standards.

Asking the Right Question

At the heart of good curriculum is asking the right questions. The quality of our study will always be related to the quality of the questions with which we engage and challenge the children.

My curriculum always begins with a question. The question gives shape to our wonderings, organizes them around a unifying principle, is the impetus for collecting and comparing observations, ideas, and experiences. The question becomes the vessel that collects and stores the results of the research and the knowledge gained in the course of a learning adventure.

The question is also the "motorvator" that runs the ship of exploration, keeps it going in the face of difficulty. It is the banner which defines our journey and by which we measure our progress. It plots the coordinates that guide our expedition. We return to it again and again, seeing how new evidence sheds light on it, refines it, deepens it. It expands as we learn more: at the end of our study will be new questions.

Good questions always cause students to think, to respond, and then to think again as their ideas are challenged by different observations, new evidence, other people's perspectives. The process of questioning, responding, and being responsible for the logical consequences of an idea helps students to refine and adapt their own conceptions. It trains them in the art of logic and reasoned thinking. A question leaves the students free to make discoveries. That is the heart of it. They are not told, but rather drawn out, educed. That is the genius of the questioning process: bringing out what is already there—ideas, hypotheses, imagination—not filling up an empty space.

Questions are at the heart of thinking. We carry on an internal dialogue that forms thoughts and then questions them. Many children do not yet engage in this inner dialogue. They need someone else to play the role of the questioner. One of our goals must be to help the students develop the habit of inner dialogue, asking questions of themselves to explore and develop their own thinking.

We also want our students to build the habit of asking questions as they encounter the world. Questions articulate our wonder. They give voice to our curiosity. They recover the extraordinary from the tomb of the taken for granted. I always tell my students about Isaac Newton. He was sitting under an apple tree and saw an apple fall to the ground. Thousands of people had witnessed the same phenomenon, but Isaac did something no one else had done. He asked a question: Why did that apple fall down? And if the apple falls down when it is freed from the tree, why doesn't the moon do likewise? These questions led him to discover the laws of physics that govern our solar system. Our students take too much for granted. Asking questions renews the obvious, helps us get to the hidden heart of the familiar. Good questions are like the kiss of the prince that awakens the beauty from sleep.

Asking questions also promotes an interest in the "Other," acting as a balance to the self-absorption and self-centeredness that so pervades our culture. I am amazed at how many people I meet are so full of themselves that they never think to ask me a question about myself or are so full of their own opinion that there is no room to grow and expand in response to an idea or perspective someone else might offer.

Questions are useful in dealing with social, moral, and discipline problems. A question that causes someone to reflect on her behavior offers the possibility of change from within rather than an imposed sanction (although that might be necessary as well). If a child destroys materials in the classroom and I tell him to stop, he may stop temporarily, but he is not changed. If I ask why he is behaving that way and get him to reflect on the consequences of his behavior, he may see the need to change himself. Then we are working *together* on transformation; I'm not working against his habits.

It is extremely important for teachers to ask the right questions, to help students formulate and articulate the right questions, and to lead the dialogue that follows from the questions, encouraging various hypotheses and testing them against further observations and the body of established knowledge in each discipline.

Elements of a Good Question

I once invited a historian to my class to speak to the children about the Pilgrims and colonial life. He gave a marvelous presentation, but I noticed that all the questions he asked were answered by the same two children, who happened to have a lot of prior knowledge about the subject. Our questions must be broad enough that all children will have an entry point. They must move away from facts toward imagination, invite hypothesis rather than factual recall.

Good questions provoke a diversity of responses. They have no one right answer. They encourage children to test their thoughts in the public arena.

Good questions matter. They deal with subject content that is meaningful and interesting. They have relevance to the students' lives.

A good question will be challenging to the community at large, no matter what the level of sophistication. It will be a question that is of interest to the teacher as well as the students. It could be asked of people of all ages. It will have entry points for the least and the most academically developed.

Some questions present a puzzle or dissonance that needs to be reconciled. Questions that elicit seemingly conflicting observations or perspectives challenge students to think in creative and imaginative ways.

The Teacher's Role

The teacher plays an important role in establishing a questioning culture in the classroom. When students are taught the habits of inquiry, any discussion may open the door to exciting learning. To promote an environment that fosters questioning, teachers

- Give students time to reflect, thus letting the questions ripen and deepen until the class is compelled to search for answers.
- Avoid the quick response; they discourage students from making quick judgments and saying the first thing that comes to mind.
- Let students speak about a question from multiple perspectives; they encourage divergent thinking while at the same time challenging students to keep to the point.
- Appreciate every thoughtful response and follow up with questions that explore the ramifications of a particular idea or point of view.

- Challenge students to explore the relationships between thoughts and to take into account other observations or data.
- Keep everyone involved, actively pursuing children who tend not to participate and challenging the superficial to dig deeper.
- Focus on the thinking behind the response, not on labeling it right or wrong; they attempt to make thinking visible.
- Celebrate the question itself! Sometimes in the middle of class, if a child asks a particularly insightful or profound question, I stop everything and call her to the front of the room for a handshake. Even if we never answer the question, we are all more thoughtful people from having heard it.

CHAPTER THREE

What Is the Ideal Classroom?

I have attended numerous workshops over the years at which various inspiring experts have described their programs for educational reform. One feature they all have in common is that the faculty are required to spend lots of time together reflecting on what is being taught and what is being learned. I wonder how many of the statistics they cite to support the validity of their programs can really be attributed to the teachers' working together in a reflective way. Give us time to reflect on our work and plan together, and teachers will make radical improvements in the education of children.

I learned firsthand the transforming power of collaboration when Debbie O'Hara, a tutor in my class, and I went to a three-day conference together. In one of the activities we were asked to design the ideal classroom. Debbie and I went to separate corners of the room to dream, and when we met to share our vision, we were shocked to find that we had independently imagined the same ideal classroom. It was empty. The children would come into an empty classroom and they would design it to meet their learning needs.

We listened at the conference as other groups proposed their ideal environments. We were tempted by the glass door opening into the Japanese garden. The hot tub in the back of the room was almost too much to resist. But when our turn came, we presented the image of the empty classroom. We described the skills that would be needed to plan, fund, and build a learning environment. The math of designing, measuring, and constructing would offer many challenges. The simple machines that are part of the tools we would use and the environmental impact of the materials we would consume fit well into our fourth-grade science curriculum. A connection could be made to the Pilgrims, a required fourth-grade social studies unit, who also came to a new environment and had to shape it to meet their needs.

Behind our idea of the empty classroom was a desire to involve the children in the planning that we usually do for them. Sometimes our efforts to organize work space and lessons for our students actually prevent them from experiencing the full measure of pride and joy in creating something out of nothing but their own imagination, perseverance, organization, and effort. We give them coloring books to fill in the lines. We give them worksheets to fill in the blanks. We give them tests to fill in the answers. In this context, the carefully organized room gives them prefabricated spaces and structures to fill in with activities.

An empty classroom seemed like the ultimate blank canvas to put before students. And since we had each thought of this idea independently, we took it as a definite sign that it was to be more than just an exercise at a conference. We felt obliged to try it in September.

The Plan

Once we decided to make it real, we began to think how we would communicate the value of the project to everyone who would be affected. How would we convince the administration that we could meet the requirements of the Lexington Public Schools? How would we share our idea with the rest of the staff at Bowman School? How would we assure parents that their children would learn all the skills expected of a fourth grader in Lexington?

We made a list of all the knowledge and skills needed to plan and build a classroom. We outlined the opportunities there would be to develop skills in math, science, reading, writing, social studies, and the arts. We described the physical activities and the challenges we would face in making decisions together as a community.

From this list we produced a document that described in fuller detail the vast opportunities this kind of learning held for the children (see Appendix A). We used this plan to demonstrate to the administration and the parents how we would cover the required Lexington curriculum in the context of our project. We met with the superintendent, our principal, and our faculty to explain the project and enlist their cooperation. The administration was supportive from the beginning; both the superintendent and the principal were encouraging. But the faculty meeting proved more problematic. Teachers had a variety of responses. Some helped us clarify our vision and adapt our plans. Others were disturbed by the unorthodox approach and how it might compare with their classes. (Appendix B identifies the main concerns raised at the faculty meeting and our responses.) The most strident opposition came from fifth-grade teachers; their objection centered on our hope to stay with the class for two years, which meant one of them would have to switch grades with us the next year. In the end, none of them was willing to do that, so it became a one-year project.

Summer Preparations

That summer, my fifteen-year-old son, who had just finished taking a business course in high school, began chastising me for having kept his money in a regular savings account. He had become aware of the possibilities the stock market offered to improve his rate of return. We began to study the market together, and he invested his savings in several stocks. My investigation of the stock market played a crucial role in how we decided to fund our project. I had previously thought of applying for a grant. But if we supplied the money, I feared we would be robbing the children of the challenge to raise it themselves. These children were too used to having things given to them anyway. What if we offered shares in a corporation? Could we get people in town to invest in our project? Could we establish this program without any money from the school system? We put out a feeler in the local newspaper, a letter to the editor briefly describing our intentions and asking anyone who might be interested in hearing more about the project in the fall to drop us a note. We also sent the letter to some businesses and town officials and asked that they send back an enclosure indicating their interest. Eighteen people and businesses wanted to find out more about the project, so there was hope.

We made the final decision to go ahead when we realized the connection to the Pilgrims. To fund their journey to a new world, the Pilgrims got local business to invest in their cause. We would do the same. In fact, we saw a close parallel between our journey and theirs. They came to an unfamiliar world and had to adapt to it and shape it to meet their needs. We would come into an empty classroom and do the same. The Pilgrims could be our model. Whenever we came to a problem, we would research whether the Pilgrims ever confronted the same issue and whether or not their course of action could inform our decision. Looking back at Pilgrim life became a refrain throughout the year. William Bradford's diary served as our primary resource about how some of our country's first European set-tlers dealt with some of the same problems we faced in our classroom challenge. We would call ourselves "Pilgrims '92."

Of course, the Pilgrims encountered an existing people and cul-ture when they arrived. The Native American experience, the focus of an in-depth study at another grade level in Lexington, was not the focal point of our project, though we did set the Pilgrims' journey in its broader historical context. Without glorifying the Pilgrim cul-ture, we studied its strengths and weaknesses in the context of the physical challenges and inner dynamics of people trying to build a community.

Once the project was definite, we met with parents whose chil-dren would be in the class. We wanted to make sure they supported the idea and to give those who did not approve an opportunity to switch their child into a different fourth-grade class. One family had concerns about the capitalist overtones they sensed in our writ-ten plan. It took us two meetings to work through the difficulties. We saw it was important to stress the idea of a *cooperative* rather than a corporation, and in the end, this proved to be an important distinction. These parents were to be among our most enthusiastic supporters.

Finally we sent a letter to the children over the summer and asked them to draw a map of their ideal classroom and bring it to school on the first day. When they arrived in Room 9 in September, they found an empty classroom.

The Year Begins

The first day of school, after expressing our initial amazement at the empty classroom, we settled into a circle and began to discuss what we were going to do. We shared our maps and began to plan how to meet the challenge of creating a learning environment with no resources but our own wits and effort. While the children's designs for the room were very interesting, all had one thing in common: they assumed that there was ample space to fit anything in—desks,

Writing letters to shareholders

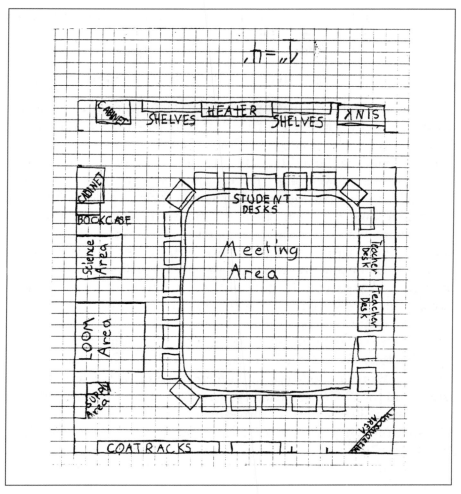

FIG. 3-1:   *Room plan redrawn to scale*

tables, work areas, meeting areas, what have you. One child even had room for a swimming pool! It was clear the first activity would be to redraw the maps according to scale. This wasn't part of our plan, but the need was obvious and the time was ripe.

Scale is a fascinating concept. You can fit the whole world on a single piece of paper. We used careful measurement, multiplication, division, fractions, and ratios to reconstruct our maps according to scale. Each child then presented his or her scale design to the class (one is shown in Figure 3–1).

The Cooperative: Involving the Community

As we compared our ideas for the classroom, our next step became clear. We had to decide what kind of work surfaces we wanted and whether we would build or buy them. The students were quick to agree on building them. I had imagined we would sit at tables for four or six, thinking fewer, larger pieces would be more manageable. But the students were passionate about having their own desks. I believe I should always try to help them accomplish their vision, but I could not imagine building twenty-three desks, and I don't like to take on a project I don't think we can achieve with high standards. I tried to convince them that the time and expense of building twenty-three individual desks would be prohibitive. They were willing to strike a compromise: we would make twelve two-person desks.

"Where are you going to get the wood? The tools?" I challenged. "You will need some money to begin. How will you get it?"

The Pilgrims provided the model. How did they finance their voyage? We read about the investment agreement between the Pilgrims and the "Merchants and Adventurers in London" in Bradford's diary. We talked about how investments were different from donations. An investor expects something back, a dividend. Did we have anything to give back to our community? The children had many ideas, from various direct services to products from our class projects: a loaf of bread from winter wheat we would grow, harvest, process, and bake; a weaving from wool we would wash, card, spin, dye, and weave; a weekly newsletter to report our progress and activities; invitations to seasonal performances of music, poetry, dance, and drama; calendars from a project in geometric construction. An investor also expects to receive the principal back, and better yet a profit, when the project is complete. We thought we could sell our assets at the end of the year to raise funds to return the investments.

But first we needed to identify local businesses or individuals who might be interested in purchasing a share. Those who had indicated interest during the summer were our first contacts. All the places in town that the children frequented—restaurants, drug stores, toy stores—were also candidates. Combing the yellow pages yielded an extensive list of potential investors. Individuals were also allowed to invest, providing they did not have any children in the school. We wanted to involve people who wouldn't ordinarily have any contact with the school so they could see some of the exciting things happening in education. The children wrote letters to all the potential investors, enticing them with dividends, and inviting them to purchase a share in our cooperative for fifty dollars (see Figure 3–2 for an example). We hoped to sell twenty shares to raise one thousand dollars.

There is nothing quite like the excitement of receiving mail in class, especially when you open it and find checks from investors. Sixteen businesses bought shares, including three banks, the neighborhood ice cream store, a hardware store, a softball team, a craft store, a Realtor, a car dealer, and a restaurant. Eighteen individuals (including a member of the Board of Selectmen) joined the cooperative; some of them were senior citizens. These thirty-four shareholders bought a total of forty-three shares. (There were other people who wanted to invest, but we were worried about being able to produce dividends for so many members, so we closed the offering. We did invite various community friends to join as honorary members.)

We had collected $2,075 in checks. What should we do with the money? The children wanted to put it in the bank, but which bank? We invited representatives from the three banks who invested to explain why we should deposit our money in their institution. One offered a higher interest rate, but would charge $1 for every transaction. Another offered lower interest, but a free account. The children had to figure out which was the best offer. They learned how interest worked and estimated the number of transactions we would conduct. They decided on the bank that offered the free account.

One of the investors was an accountant, so we invited her in to teach us how to set up the books and keep careful records of our financial activities. The accounting throughout the year offered rich

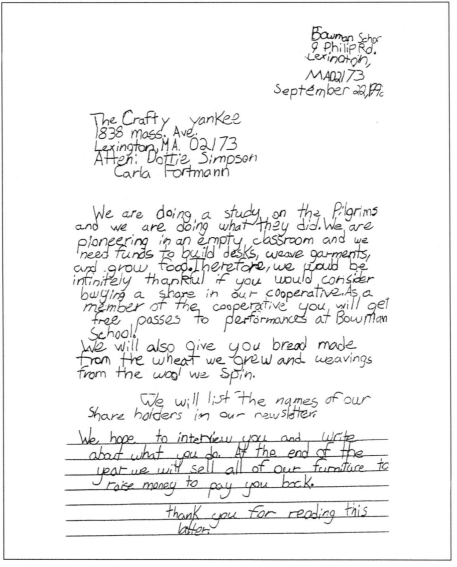

Bowman Schor
9 Philip Rd.
Lexington,
MA 02173
September 22, 89c

The Crafty Yankee
1838 Mass. Ave.
Lexington, M.A. 02173
Atten: Dottie Simpson
Carla Fortmann

We are doing a study on the Pilgrims and we are doing what they did. We are pioneering in an empty classroom and we need funds to build desks, weave garments, and grow food. Therefore, we would be infinitely thankful if you would consider buying a share in our cooperative. As a member of the cooperative you will get free passes to performances at Bowman School!
We will also give you bread made from the wheat we grew and weavings from the wool we spin.

We will list the names of our share holders in our newsletter.

We hope to interview you and write about what you do. At the end of the year we will sell all of our furniture to raise money to pay you back.

thank you for reading this letter.

FIG. 3-2: *Letter to potential shareholder*

Dear Shareholder,

During the first quarter of Pilgrims '92 we have sold shares to 16 businesses, and 18 individuals. We also have 9 honorary members. The total is 43 shareholders.

Unicef

With some of our money we have sent seeds to Mali's villages in Africa to help build better futures.

Desks

We have selected our wood and have completed 6 desks and have a 7th on the way. We plan to finish 12 by the end of 1992.

Expenses

Loom	325.00
Printing	8.93
wheat berries	22.60
wood	154.34
Unicef	128.00
Printing	12.34
bread supplies	54.22
Total	$705.43

Liabilities

Mr. Cassell (wood)	75.18
Mr. Levy (printing)	11.76
Total liabilities	86.94
Total Expenses + Liabilities	$792.37

Assets

Deposits	2025.00	50.00
Cash		
desks (100 each)	600.00	
wood		100.00
loom		325.00
Total Assets	3100.00	
Networth	$2307.63	

We thank you again for showing your interest in Pilgrims '92 and hope to see you soon.

Sincerely,
Pilgrims '92

FIG. 3-3:   *Quarterly report*

opportunities to learn and practice our math skills. We calculated our finances weekly, and issued quarterly statements for the investors (see Figure 3–3).

Building the Desks

Now we returned to the furniture design. One of our shareholders, Mr. Cassell, was a craftsman, so we invited him to our class to discuss our furniture needs and help us develop a design for our desks. We determined how big the surface area needed to be for two people to work comfortably. We wanted a design that would allow us to flip the top of the desks vertically so we could store them against the wall when we needed open space in the classroom. Mr. Cassell showed us designs for desks that might have been used by the Pilgrims. We chose a design and Mr. Cassell built us a scale model. We constructed a

My Dearest Friends,

Mr. Cassell and I will be going to the lumber yard this weekend. We need your guidance to determine how much of each size to get. We would also like to know how much it will cost. Will we have enough with our $400?

Here are the lumber prices:

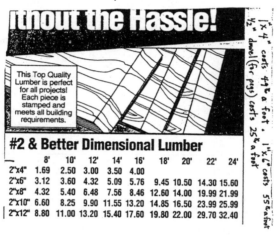

ithout the Hassle!

This Top Quality Lumber is perfect for all projects! Each piece is stamped and meets all building requirements.

1"x 4" costs 49¢ a foot. 1"x 6" costs 55¢ a foot. ½" dowel (for pegs) costs 25¢ a foot

#2 & Better Dimensional Lumber

	8'	10'	12'	14'	16'	18'	20'	22'	24'
2"x4"	1.69	2.50	3.00	3.50	4.00				
2"x6"	3.12	3.60	4.32	5.09	5.76	9.45	10.50	14.30	15.60
2"x8"	4.32	5.40	6.48	7.56	8.46	12.60	14.00	19.99	21.99
2"x10"	6.60	8.25	9.90	11.55	13.20	14.85	16.50	23.99	25.99
2"x12"	8.80	11.00	13.20	15.40	17.60	19.80	22.00	29.70	32.40

Here is the lumber we need according to measurements of our scale model. The numbers are the wood we need for 1 desk.

size	amount we need	number of pieces
2" x 4"	1' 6"	2
2" x 6"	2' 4"	2
1" x 4"	1' 6"	1
1" x 4"	1' 9"	1
1" x 6"	1'	2

FIG. 3-4: *Figuring out what size lumber to buy*

Look at the column marked 2"x4". You will notice that an 8' piece will cost $1.69, a 10' piece will cost $2.50, etc. We need 2"x4" cut in pieces 1'6" long. The question is,, shall we buy the 8' piece, the 10' piece or the 12' piece? Does it make any difference? If so, why?

Give us your recommendations:
What size 2"x4" shall we buy? 12'

Explain why: The Length of the peice We need is 1'6" and $1\frac{1}{2} \times 2 = 3$ So Counting by. Shows that We get 8 1'6" Peices w/no Leftovers.

What size 2"x6" shall we buy? 10'

Explain why The Length of the peice We need is 2'4" and $2'4" \times 2 = 48" \times 2 = 96"$ So there is only a 4" left over.

How much will the 2"x4's^cost to make 12 desks $9.00
Show how you got your answer below.

1 Plank of 12' = 4 Desk Feet
3 Planks of 12' = 12 Desk feet
$3.00 × 3 = $9.00

FIG. 3-4   *continued*

prototype, proposed some modifications, and finalized a design. We decided to use hand tools and pegs for construction, because that's the way the Pilgrims would have done it. The students would build the desks (and later the chairs) during project time (an hour at the end of the day) and any free time (before school, after school, and during recess).

Planning, buying, and cutting the wood offered many real-life mathematical challenges. For example, our desk tops were to measure two feet by three feet. Plywood comes in sheets four feet by eight feet. How many sheets do we need to build twelve desks? How will we cut the wood to have the least amount of waste and the most useful shapes left over to use in another project? Two-by-fours come in lengths of six, eight, ten, twelve, fourteen, or sixteen feet. We want to cut feet for the desk legs that are eighteen inches long. What length of two-by-four can be cut into eighteen-inch sections without any waste? (The two-by-four problem is part of the larger problem shown in Figure 3–4.)

Problems like these are always more motivating and interesting than abstract ones from a book. The children are motivated because getting the right answer really counts. Real business transactions will be undertaken based on their calculations. Problems like this also have more than one possible solution. For example, in the plywood problem, most of the children figured out we could cut five two-foot-by-three-foot pieces from each sheet of plywood. Theodore's answer was four pieces from each, so I called him over to my desk to show him how he could cut a fifth piece if he rotated the board. He said, "Yeah, I saw that, but I figured whether you cut four or five pieces, you will still need three sheets of plywood for twelve desks. By cutting only four tops from each sheet you will have larger and more useful pieces left over." (See Figure 3–5.) To solve the two-by-four problem, the children cut paper models of the different lengths to scale and cut them in pieces to see which could be cut evenly. They worked with great precision, because their own money was at stake.

Staining the wood offered another great mathematical challenge. After we had constructed the desks, we had to figure out how much stain we needed to buy to finish them (see Figure 3–6). The class

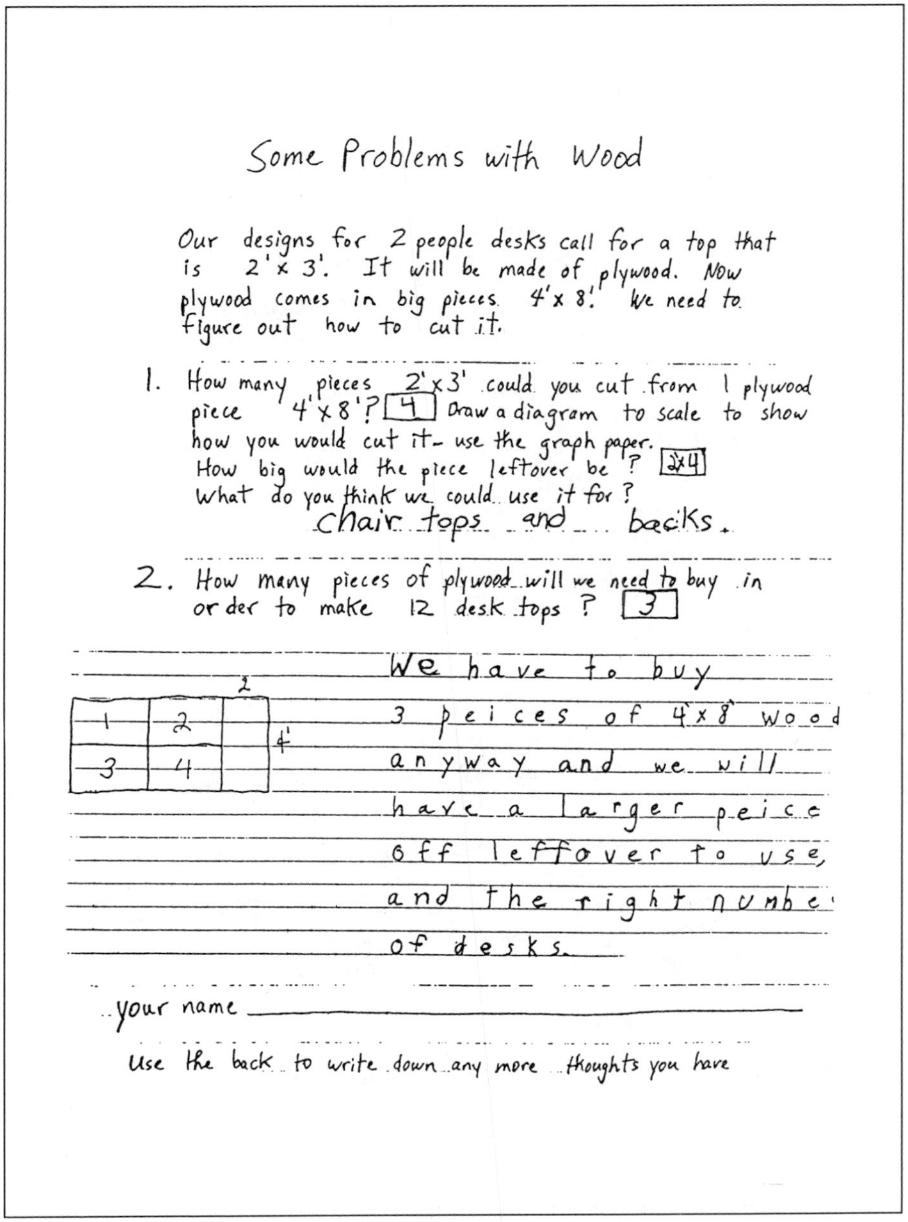

Some Problems with Wood

Our designs for 2 people desks call for a top that is 2' × 3'. It will be made of plywood. Now plywood comes in big pieces 4' × 8'. We need to figure out how to cut it.

1. How many pieces 2' × 3' could you cut from 1 plywood piece 4' × 8'? ☐4 Draw a diagram to scale to show how you would cut it — use the graph paper. How big would the piece leftover be? ☐2×4 What do you think we could use it for?
   Chair tops and backs.

2. How many pieces of plywood will we need to buy in order to make 12 desk tops? ☐3

1	2	
3	4	

We have to buy 3 peices of 4 × 8 wood anyway and we will have a larger peice off leftover to use, and the right number of desks.

your name _____

Use the back to write down any more thoughts you have

FIG. 3-5: *Student's calculation of what size wood to buy*

Finishing the Desks

1-4-73

A _Finish_ is applied to the surface to protect from soiling or stains. It seals the pores in the wood and hardens for protection. Finishing also brings out the color in the wood, or even changes the color if desired.

We will be using a fine finish called WATCO Danish Oil Finish. We have to figure out how much to buy. The figures below will help you decide.

WATCO comes in 3 sizes: pint, quart and gallon.
2 pints = 1 quart
4 quarts = 1 gallon

1 pint covers about 30 square ft.
1 quart covers about 60 square ft.
1 gallon covers about 240 square ft.

The prices are as follows:
1 pint = $ 6.30
1 quart = $ 8.40
1 gallon = $19.80

Your job is to figure out how much oil we should buy to cover all the desks (tops and bottoms) at the least possible expense.

There are 4 people in each group. The director organizes the project and encourages everyone to participate with their best effort. The measurer holds the ruler and makes all measurements. The calculator holds the calculator and computes all numbers. The recorder records all data and * writes report to present to the class. Make sure to record your data carefully! Check your figures twice! Decide when to estimate or round-off and when you must be precise.

* Everyone helps decide what to say - the reporter does the writing.

FIG. 3-6: *Calculating how much stain to buy*

54

worked in small groups measuring the surface area of the desks, which included rectangles, trapezoids, and cylinders. They had to measure tops, bottoms, and edges because the whole thing would be stained. They had to translate square inches to square feet (not by dividing by twelve, as many of them thought!). I gave them brochures telling how many square feet would be covered by a pint, quart, or gallon of stain. One group, in an attempt to be as thrifty as possible, figured we needed one gallon, one quart, and one pint. They were shocked to find that the cost for their recommendation would be considerably more than another group's recommendation of two gallons. A great lesson in the economy of purchasing in quantity!

Rhythm of the Day

I ordered the school day so that my students did the work most intellectually demanding in the morning and most physically active the last thing in the afternoon. The day was divided into four main parts. We began each morning with music and poetry recitation as a segue into a ninety-minute period I called *theme time*. We focused on the analytical and creative aspects of the project during theme time— thinking, planning, writing, reviewing, researching, making decisions. Theme time was interdisciplinary; the work might be focused on different subjects depending on the present need. The second half of the morning was reserved for skills. If I noticed that the children did not know the proper form for writing letters to the investors, I taught them this skill. If we had to make a decision about which bank to put our money in and I saw they didn't understand interest, I explained it and gave them an opportunity to explore it and apply the concept in other situations. If they needed to learn skills, primarily in math and language arts, that did not relate directly to the project, we practiced them then. (Children receiving extra help outside the classroom received it during skill time, not theme time.) After lunch we had a forty-five-minute reading time. Sometimes the literature related to the theme, but more often it did not. Then the last hour and fifteen minutes was hands-on time. Different groups of children worked on different things. Some built desks, others wrote the newsletter, still others worked with wool or wheat, figuring out how it gets from raw form to finished product. (Both wheat and wool had been major themes in previous years. They are described in Chapter 7. The year of Pilgrims '92 they became smaller projects incorporated into our major theme as dividends for the shareholders.)

Consensus

We made all our decisions by consensus. We sat in a circle on the floor, and each person had a chance to state an opinion or pass. After all opinions were heard, students were invited to defend their idea or to explain how their opinion had been modified by what they heard from their classmates. Most discussions were very civil, and consensus was clear. Sometimes the discussions were more passionate, and it took longer to make a decision. This was often the case when I proposed spending our funds to buy things. I was not reluctant to spend our money, thinking we could sell our assets at the end of the year and get it back. But the children never wanted to spend money on something they could get in some other way. Instead of our buying tools, those who could brought in tools from home. When we needed a vacuum cleaner (so we could clean up our own considerable messes and not provoke our custodian), they made an appeal through the newsletter and got one donated.

The only time the children wanted to spend our money was to help someone in need, and then they were extravagant. Once we read that people in Mali had been forced to eat their seed crop because of famine. UNICEF offered a program where one could buy seeds for the people of Mali. Each package had enough seeds to sustain a whole village. One package contained common grains, another particular seeds unique to the African climate. Should we send the common grains or the African ones? After much debate, the children were still divided. Then one child said, "Let's send them one of each!" Everyone cheered. Another said, "Let's send *two* of each!" More cheers. We also sent them a bag of seeds harvested from our own wheat garden.

Another time we read in the newspaper that a teacher in Boston

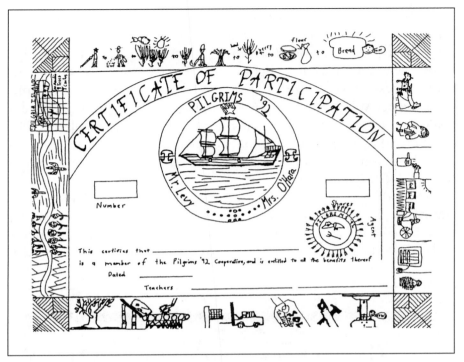

FIG. 3-7: *Hand-drawn stock certificate issued to shareholders*

who used music extensively in his kindergarten class had had his keyboard and tape recorder stolen. The children found the number of the school where the teacher taught, called him, and offered to send money to replace the equipment. In return they asked for a tape of his children singing.

The class community is forged as we learn to reconcile individual differences. Learning when to set aside our own opinion for the sake of the group and when to fight for what we believe in is a discernment we refine all of our lives. Sometimes decisions were held up because people felt strongly about their point of view. It was especially exciting when in the midst of ponderous debate, someone would have an idea that would break the stalemate. For example, we had to design a stock certificate for our shareholders. One of the investors was a stockbroker, so we invited him in to show us what certificates looked like. He brought in the certificates of various companies (the New England Patriots certificate made a big hit) and we learned what all the numbers and symbols represented. Then each child designed his or her own certificate for Pilgrims '92. A committee was formed to take the best elements from all the designs and incorporate them into a certificate. While the group was working, another child designed a beautiful and very official-looking certificate on the computer. His design sparked one of the most serious debates of the year: which to use, the hand-drawn one (Figure 3–7) or the computer creation (Figure 3–8)?

Most of the children thought the investors would prefer the computer design because it looked so official. But there was an unyielding lobby for the hand-drawn one. It represented many hours of hard work, and besides, the Pilgrims would never have used a

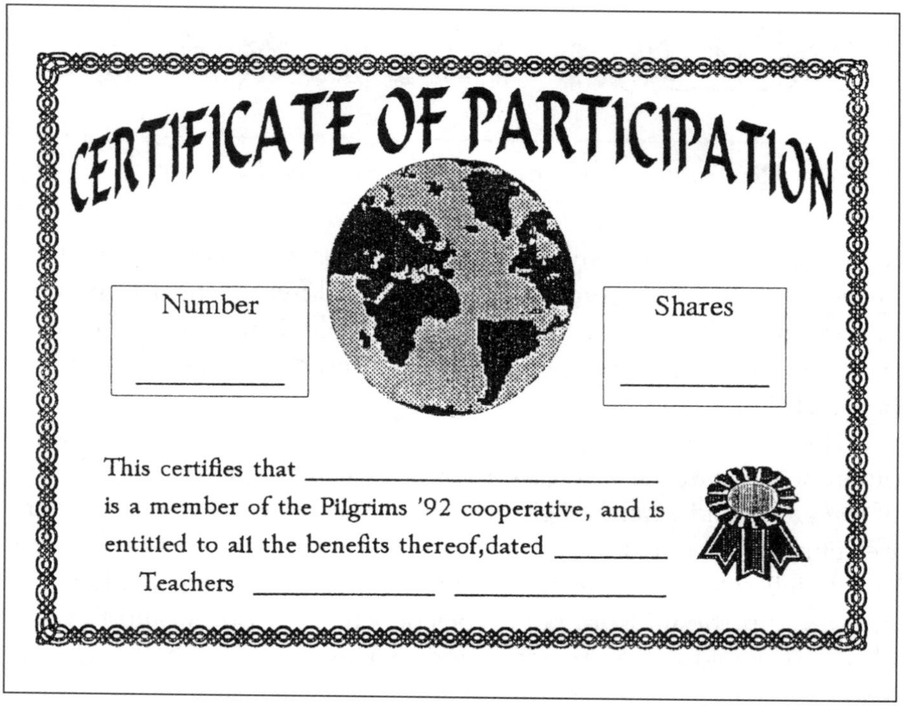

FIG. 3-8: *Computer-made stock certificate*

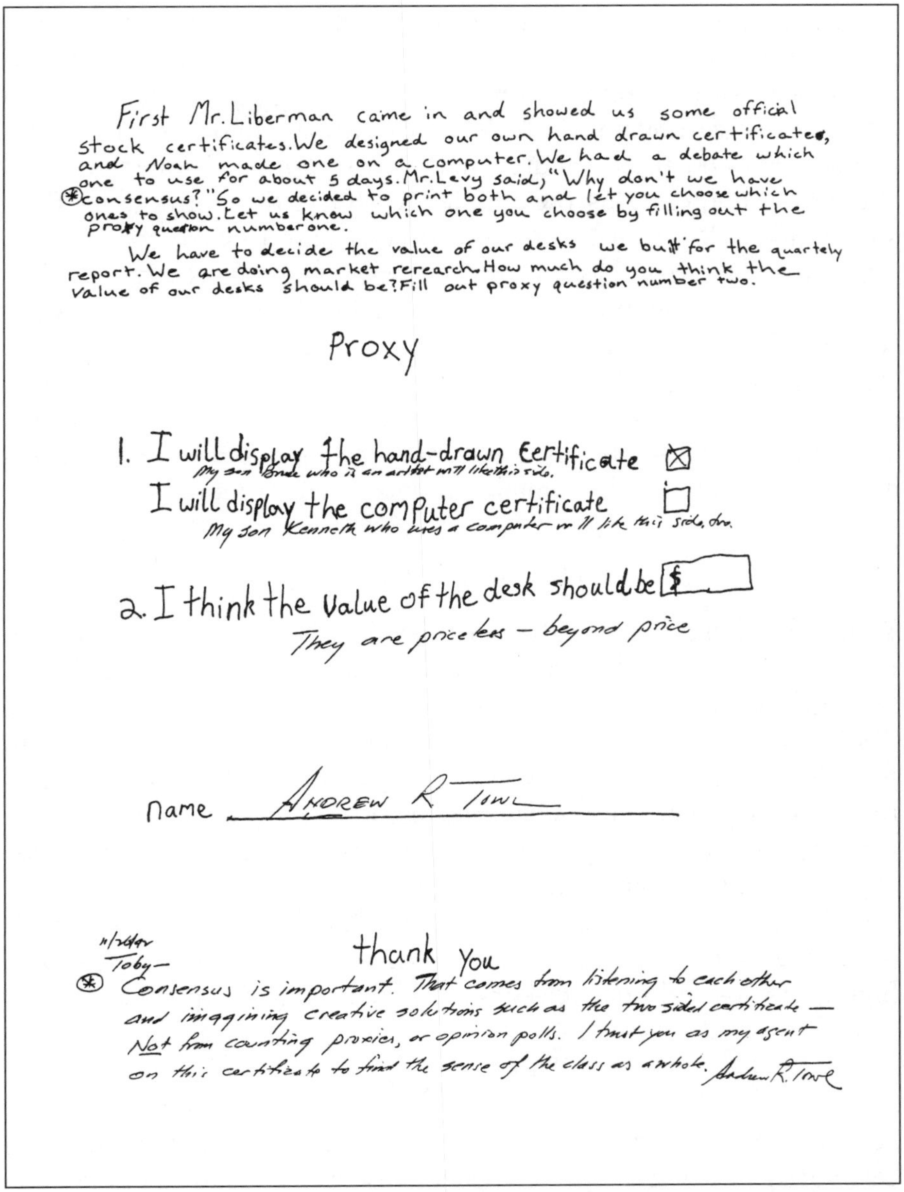

First Mr. Liberman came in and showed us some official stock certificates. We designed our own hand drawn certificates, and Noah made one on a computer. We had a debate which one to use for about 5 days. Mr. Levy said, "Why don't we have *consensus?" So we decided to print both and let you choose which ones to show. Let us know which one you choose by filling out the proxy question number one.

We have to decide the value of our desks we built for the quarterly report. We are doing market rereach. How much do you think the value of our desks should be? Fill out proxy question number two.

Proxy

1. I will display the hand-drawn Eertificate ⊠
   My son Brad who is an artist will like this side.
   I will display the computer certificate ☐
   My son Kenneth who uses a computer will like this side, chor.

2. I think the Value of the desk should be $☐
   They are priceless — beyond price

Name _ANDREW R TOWL_

thank You

⊛ Consensus is important. That comes from listening to each other and imagining creative solutions such as the two sided certificate — Not from counting proxies, or opinion polls. I trust you as my agent on this certificate to find the sense of the class as a whole. *Andrew R Towl*

FIG. 3-9: *Proxy to determine which certificate is favored, and to help establish value of desks*

computer. The few who preferred the hand-drawn certificate felt too strongly to give in. I couldn't see how we were going to find consensus and was about to call for a vote, when one of the children suggested we print the certificate on thick stock, with the hand-drawn version on one side and the computer image on the other. Fantastic! I told them how corporations use proxies to solicit the opinions of their shareholders. We sent the two-sided certificate to each shareholder, along with a proxy (see Figure 3–9) asking them which side they intended to display. We also used the proxy for some market research to determine the value of a completed desk for accounting purposes. As I had hoped, all the shareholders said they liked the hand-drawn side better. This was a valuable lesson to the children. Even though something that uses the latest technology may look more polished and professional, the handmade product is much more valuable.

The Desk Olympics

When the desks were finally constructed, we celebrated with a ceremony that lasted all day. In the morning we sang songs that had been written for the occasion and recited poems and stories about the desks. Special songs honored Mr. Cassell, our craftsman, and Mr. Ritchie, a retired gentleman who came in many afternoons to help the children build. Dances demonstrated the movements of the tools we used in construction. Finally, in a long-anticipated moment, we all sat down together for the first time.

The afternoon was given over to the "Desk Olympics." The children invented many contests involving the desks—high jumps over, limbo under—and other classroom challenges (see Appendix C).

The Auction

At the end of the year we invited the shareholders and parents to a celebration with dinner, closing ceremonies, and an auction. The children recited a class poem they had written about the year (see Appendix D). The most exciting part of the evening was the auction. One of the principles of investing is that the investors have the right at any time to sell their shares and receive their portion of the assets.

Desks—before and after finishing

At the beginning of the year we had promised the shareholders that we would return their investment to them at the end of the year. We planned to do this by liquidating all our assets.

We had also studied how the value of something was determined by the law of supply and demand, so throughout the year we had a little "museum" of items of value to the citizens of Room 9. These included the confetti gathered from the holes we punched in binding our geometric calendars; some wheat seeds left over from our wheat harvest; some wool left over from our weaving project; knitting needles we made from wooden dowels; a framed leaf, the last one hanging on the oak tree outside our window, a tree we'd written about all year. We put these items on the auction block. Children took turns being the auctioneer, and by the end of the night they could rattle off the customary "I've got five, who'll give me ten?" with the best of them.

We'd raffled off one desk to someone in the school; another to

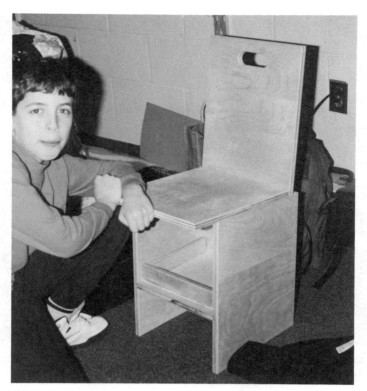

Chairs were built after desks

someone in our class. After three of the remaining desks were sold to the highest bidders at the auction, we'd raised enough money to pay back all the investors. That meant we still had seven desks. We could have sold them and made a handsome (100 percent) profit for the shareholders. But the shareholders voted to return them to the class. Six were taken home by children chosen by lot, and the seventh desk remains in my classroom as a monument to the momentous voyage of Pilgrims '92.

Beyond the obvious benefits of financial support, our partnership with the community gave the children a tremendous sense of motivation to excel in their work. Learning was released from the confines of the classroom and set free to explore the world. The partnership gave the children something their parents and teachers could never provide. Children *expect* parents and teachers to be interested in their activities. But the interest from the businesses and citizens of our community was completely unexpected. It inspired our gratitude and motivated us to work hard in everything we did. It also gave the community a firsthand glimpse of what is happening in our schools and opened up possibilities for future involvement. In fact, one of our investors went on to join our site-based council. At the end of the year, when we attempted to return the investments to the shareholders, most of them asked us to keep the funds for a new project the following year. But that's another story (see Chapter 9).

Making History While We Study It

Throughout the whole year, we were aware that we were making history at the same time we studied it. We were able to learn about the Pilgrims because William Bradford had written a diary. How would people three hundred years from today know anything about what our lives were like? The weekly newsletters were one way we reflected and reported on our story. But unlike the Pilgrims, we also had technology that could record images to show future generations what our lives were like. We decided to make a video with the help of an extraordinarily dedicated and talented parent, who videotaped throughout the year and took groups of children to the high school to help her edit. The children wrote the script. (This video is also available from Heinemann.)

Reflections

The following year students, parents, and other teachers walked by my class in September, astonished to see traditional desks set in rows. "Mr. Levy's room with desks in rows?!" they exclaimed. I tried to explain that the desks didn't really matter. It doesn't have anything to do with how you arrange your desks or how you design your room. What really counts is the relationship between the teacher and the class, the kind of community that is forged between people. The reason I feel confident to undertake such bold activities with such unknown outcomes is that I know my relationship with the children and the quality of the community we will build together will be strong enough to overcome any obstacle.

"But won't you do this project again?" they inquire. No, I suspect not. For one thing, a project like this requires a tremendous amount of help from many other people. I would hesitate to ask them all to do it again. Their help came freely and with joy the first time, and I would hate to risk seeing it become an obligation. On a more personal note, I would not do it again for the same reason an artist would not paint the same picture again, or a musician would not compose the same piece of music again. Teaching is an art. A project like this is better framed as a unique creation of all the individuals who worked to make it happen: students, teachers, parents, and community members. Each year brings together a new configuration of people with a unique calling, unlike any that has gone before. I listen for it every year.

CHAPTER FOUR

Was the American Revolution Completed Before the War Began?

I am required by the Lexington Public Schools to teach the American Revolution as part of my fourth-grade social studies curriculum. There are textbooks that predictably recount the acts and tariffs imposed by the British, the reactions of the colonists, the succession of battles, and the eventual winning of our independence. There is some value in learning these facts. They become part of the national lore that we share as Americans. But if we stop with the "tit for tat" events that culminated in a war, our students will gain only the most superficial understanding of what the American Revolution was about. I wanted to inspire my students to find out what the revolution meant, the part it played in the evolution of our civilization, and its relevance to their own lives. I needed a question that would open the door to understanding on a deeper level. My first step was to read about the American Revolution myself.

Finding the Grand Question

In my reading, a jewel of a question gleamed in a letter by John Adams. It promised to open the many facets of exploration and discovery that would lead us to the deeper aspects of what the revolution was about. Adams wrote in 1818, "The Revolution was completed before the war ever commenced. The real American Revolution was in the minds and hearts of the people. Their changing opinions, values and sentiments, that was the real American Revolution." What did he mean by this perplexing paradox: the Revolution completed before the war ever began?! This incongruity is the kind of puzzle that can be reconciled only from deep levels of understanding. What was changing in the minds and hearts of the people? is the kind of grand question that launches a complex investigation. Grand questions like this have no single right or wrong answer. They compel viewing the topic from multiple perspectives. They lead us back to original documents in our research. They provide opportunities for the students to develop skills and master content in the course of the investigation.

When I asked my students what they thought of when they heard the words *American Revolution*, I heard nothing but images of "soldiers," "Redcoats," "muskets," "Paul Revere," "'the rockets' red glare, the bombs bursting in air.'" So when I put this quotation from John Adams before them, they were quite puzzled. They had only a vague idea what Adams was talking about. The vocabulary was new for most of them, and the concepts quite sophisticated. I gave them words like *revolution, sentiments, affections, opinions,* and *commenced* for their spelling words the first week. They learned the definitions and wrote the words in sentences.

Then I told them their challenge was to figure out what John Adams meant. I thought this approach would lead them to discover the genius of the American Revolution, which I saw emerging in the tension between authority and freedom, between dependence on the powers that be and the desire to decide for oneself. All the ways that we might see the American Revolution, all the lenses that highlight different aspects of it, share the development of a powerful sense of self. In the late eighteenth century, the importance and value of the individual was supplanting the prevailing loyalty to the established hierarchies of authority and power. A person's identity was beginning to be expressed as an individual rather than through the authorities to which he or she was subject.

Learning from the Past

What was changing in the minds and hearts of the people? To explore this change, we looked back to the preceding centuries to see what the relationships were like between the individual and the authorities. We took a brief look at medieval life, in which the common people were totally bound by the political, economic, and religious governance of the feudal system. There was no room for individual expression. From there we went on to study the lives of leading personalities from the Renaissance. Of particular interest were persons whose lives reflected the genius of the times. Where could we find seeds of this new sense of self, of the value and dignity of the individual, that would flower in the ideals of the American Revolution? Galileo stood out in science, Martin Luther and Joan of Arc in religion, Oliver Cromwell in politics, and Leonardo da Vinci in the arts. Their biographies are vivid illustrations of individuals who stood up against the authorities, championed new frontiers, and paid a significant price. They demonstrated on a personal level the dramatic change in the minds and hearts of the people that would later be manifest in society, where individual dignity and independence became prizes worth dying for.

First I told my class about Galileo, who was born in Pisa, Italy, in 1564. As a child, he loved to tinker, making little toys with levers and pulleys that fascinated his sisters. As a young man he wanted to be a monk. However, his father hoped Galileo would become rich and replenish the dwindling family fortune, so he sent him to medical school to become a doctor. The school was torture for Galileo. His impatience made it difficult for him to listen to his teachers, who taught by lecture and demonstration. He frequently questioned the facts they taught him. "Why is this so? What would happen if we treated the patient this way instead of that?" His teachers would tell him, "This is always the way it has been done. We do not ask why." Galileo was expelled for his constant questioning.

Galileo left the school and went into a nearby church. I let the children imagine his thoughts at this time. He must have been terribly worried about how his father would react. He may have returned to his boyhood dreams of becoming a monk. But while he was in the church, he watched the priests come by and swing the great incense lamps that hung on long chains from the ceiling. He noticed that no matter how far the incense lamps were swung, it took the exact same time for them to make one complete arc. Aristotle had said that the longer arc would take a longer time. "Aha!" he shouted. "Aristotle was wrong! And now I can prove it!" Here I asked the children how they thought Galileo might have measured the swinging lamp.

"With a clock," someone said.

"That would have been very handy, but alas, they had no clocks in Galileo's time."

"He counted," someone else surmised. I had them close their eyes and count up to thirty. We noted how much time it took. Then we did it again and found it took a different amount of time.

"Counting is good. It gives us a good approximation of the time. But it might not be precise enough for Galileo to use to prove Aristotle was wrong."

"Maybe he had a sand-dial type watch."

"Well, that would give an accurate measure of a longer period of time, but would he be able to use it to measure the few seconds of the lamp's arc?"

"Maybe there was music in the church and he used the beat of the music." I love the ideas the children come up with.

"Ingenious, but alas, there was no music in the church that day."

Eventually, with a hint or two, they got it. Medical student that he was, Galileo timed the arc with his pulse. This led into a fascinating discussion of time and how it can be measured. Why can I use the sun but not the wind? Why isn't counting accurate? What is it about time, anyway? Why can I use my pulse but not my breathing? One child disputed using the pulse. She said Galileo's heartbeat would change because of his excitement at proving Aristotle wrong!

I challenged the children to design an experiment that would prove whether Galileo or Aristotle was correct, first teaching them the proper procedure for writing up a scientific experiment. They conducted their experiments, and we compared results (one group's documentation of their experiment is shown in Figure 4–1).

The students were very accurate in their measurements, using a stopwatch that showed results in hundredths of a second. One group listed their results: the long arc took 2.52 seconds; the small arc took 2.47 seconds. I was pleased—the results confirmed that the two arcs took the same amount of time—so I was shocked to hear their

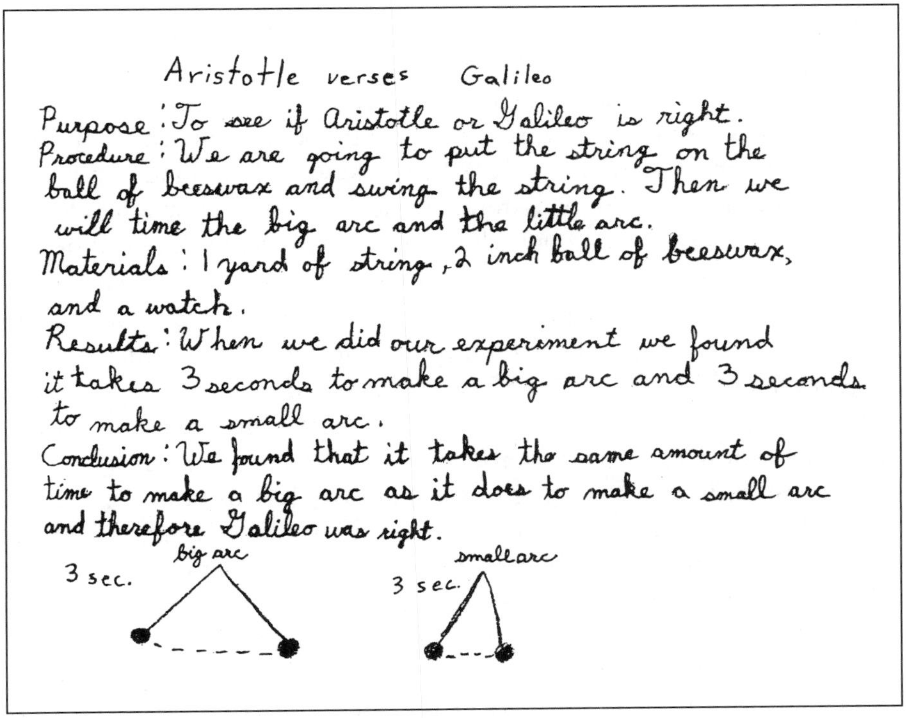
Aristotle verses Galileo
Purpose: To see if Aristotle or Galileo is right.
Procedure: We are going to put the string on the ball of beeswax and swing the string. Then we will time the big arc and the little arc.
Materials: 1 yard of string, 2 inch ball of beeswax, and a watch.
Results: When we did our experiment we found it takes 3 seconds to make a big arc and 3 seconds to make a small arc.
Conclusion: We found that it takes the same amount of time to make a big arc as it does to make a small arc and therefore Galileo was right.

FIG. 4-1: *Experiment to determine if Galileo or Aristotle was correct*

conclusion: Aristotle was correct. It did take longer for the long arc. While I naturally attributed the slight variance of .05 seconds to the imprecision of fourth-grade technique and measurement, the children took the results literally (or do we say, in this instance, mathematically?). They were being much more scientific than I. We all have a tendency to see results in terms of the outcomes we expect. On many occasions I have seen students ignore the actual results and record instead what they think the answer should be. I stood condemned by this same inclination. This led us into an important discussion about the variables that we could not precisely control, and how all measurement is approximate to the degree our instrument can measure. We learned the concept of "margin of error." We also learned why it was important to repeat an experiment multiple times and determine averages in order to get more accurate results. In this way I was able to teach the methods and skills of scientific procedure in an authentic context, one that arose from our own activity and experience.

After his epiphany, Galileo rushed out of the cathedral and set up a laboratory in which to prove Aristotle was wrong. He conducted many experiments; this was remarkable because the whole idea of doing experiments to find out what was true was heretofore unknown. Galileo is regarded as the father of modern experimental science. Before Galileo, if you wanted to find out what was true you looked in the books of Aristotle, the unquestioned authority. But this did not satisfy Galileo. He would not base his understanding on what the authorities said. He had to find out for himself! He represents in the scientific world this spirit of the individual that we would trace to our ancestors in the founding of our country. Just as Galileo insisted on finding the truth for himself, the English colonists insisted on being part of the process that would formulate the laws of our land.

I went on to recap the rest of Galileo's life. (I tell the story rather than have the children read about it. If knowledge is dependent on reading, then the children will have unequal access to it. I have books available for those who want to go into more detail, but I don't want to hinder the less able readers from taking part in the discussions and activities.) If Aristotle was wrong about the pendulum, what else might he be wrong about? Galileo staged a public demonstration from the (not yet leaning) tower of Pisa. He dropped a heavy ball and a light ball from the tower as all the professors, religious authorities, and curious townspeople watched. Sure as the eye can see, both balls hit the ground at the same time.

Nevertheless, the authorities still did not believe him, even though they had seen it with their own eyes! Aristotle had said that a heavier weight would fall faster than a lighter weight. What Aristotle said was their truth! Their conceptions were so inflexible there was no room to adjust them in the light of new data.

The children were quick to reprove the authorities for their stubborn rigidity. "I mean, they saw it, how could they not believe it?" But we always have to be careful in judging others, especially across the centuries. Is there anything we have today that we can see with our own eyes but still refuse to believe? How about magic? We cannot believe the tricks some magicians are able to perform, even though we see them with our own eyes. So it was not so unusual for the authorities to dismiss Galileo's experiment on the grounds of magic: it was an understandable hypothesis given the context in which they lived and thought. Just as we know a magician doesn't really saw a woman in half, they knew that the ideas of Aristotle and the church could not really be wrong.

The children were outraged to learn that Galileo was called to trial for his ideas and that his books were burned. They were disappointed that he recanted at the trial and admitted that all his books were false. They were thrilled that students came to visit him while he was under house arrest and smuggled his manuscripts out to other countries to be published. The truth can never die! (The story ends in 1992, when the church formally admitted it made an error in condemning Galileo and issued an official apology and pardon.)

After Galileo, we turned our attention to Martin Luther. I told the story of his life in the same way I had with Galileo's. Luther insisted that there need be no higher authority to mediate the relationship between humanity and God, that every individual needed to develop his or her own relationship with the Creator. He translated the Bible into German so the people could read it and interpret it for themselves. Luther wrote ninety-five theses detailing the errors and hypocrisies he saw in the church, and he, like Galileo, was brought to trial for his beliefs. The children were especially heartened to hear that Luther retained his conviction at his trial. Their longing to champion the courage of humanity, dampened by Galileo's retraction, was restored by Luther's refusal to recant. I had them memorize his response to the court, the heart of which is, "I cannot and will not retract anything. It is neither safe nor right to go against one's conscience. Here I stand. I cannot do otherwise. God help me. Amen." This is the same rock the American patriots stood on almost three hundred years later.

In politics, we studied Oliver Cromwell and the Glorious Revolution. The "Roundheads," as Cromwell's followers were called, were not willing to accept laws, believe laws to be righteous, just because they came from the hand of the king. They wanted to have a say in the making of those laws. We experienced their struggle in deciding whether or not to revolt against King Charles. He clearly refused to share his power with anyone, but what about the precedent set if the people seized power? What authority would ever again be safe?

The night before the king's execution Charles and his enemies prepared themselves for the final struggle. For Charles, the only victory left was in dying bravely. His enemies hoped to weaken his courage. Each side was fighting for the minds and hearts of the people. If Charles winced even a little, if by his behavior on the scaffold he showed himself unworthy of the thousands who had died defending him, the throne would be tarnished forever.

The king wore two shirts on the day of his execution to avoid the appearance of being fearful if he shivered in the cold January morning. Cromwell had moved the crowd far enough away from the scaffold so they would not be able to hear anything the king said. Nevertheless, Charles spoke, ending his remarks with a summary of his political philosophy. "For the people, and truly I desire their liberty and freedom as much as anybody, but I must tell you that their liberty and freedom consists in having, of government, those laws by which their life and their goods may be most their own. It is not for having a share in the government, sirs; that is nothing pertaining to them." To the end, Charles stood by his own ideas of government. It was for the king to decide what was good for his people. The people had no business sharing in the government.

The ax fell, and parliament tried to rule. But in a few years the people demanded a king once again, and Charles II came back from France to rule. Although certain individuals were ready for a new kind of government, the general public had not yet broken free from their dependence on the king.

Finally, in the arts we saw the rise of the individual reflected in paintings. Before this time, the subjects of art were primarily religious or royal. In the paintings of Brueghel and Leonardo the common peasant began to emerge as a worthwhile subject.

In addition to these in-class examples, I had the children read other biographies of the Renaissance in search of more examples of the changing minds and hearts of the people.

Evaluating What They Learned

I was able to evaluate the children in a variety of ways. I learned a lot about their understanding through their participation in class discussions. The children all wrote biographies of a Renaissance person that concluded with a paragraph on how this person relates to the spirit of the American Revolution (see Figure 4–2). At the

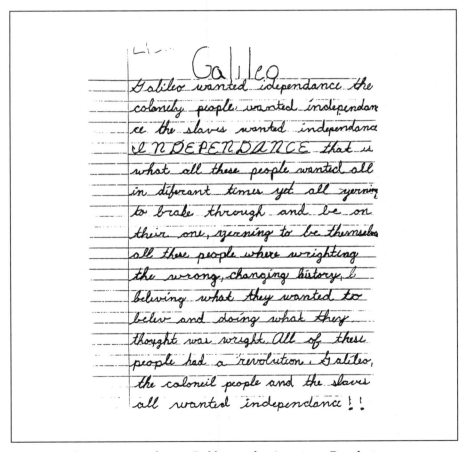

FIG. 4-2: *Composition relating Galileo to the American Revolution*

end of our study, they all wrote about what they thought John Adams meant by his statement. Emily's response represents the understanding I hoped they'd come to:

The Real American Revolution

John Adams said that the American Revolution started in the minds of the people long before the war of independence.

Before King Charles I, people believed that the royal family was blessed by God. During King Charles I's time the people were beginning to question the idea of the king having special powers to rule. Did they really need a king to rule over them?

This was happening in religion also. A monk named Martin Luther helped people form the idea that Pope and priest were not the only ones who could have a relationship with God. They thought they should be able to read the Bible for themselves and decide what it meant for themselves.

A century before the American Revolution, old ideas in science were being questioned also. Aristotle had been the greatest scientist in the world for hundreds of years, until Galileo, a young scientist, proved some of Aristotle's works wrong. But finally he was forced into saying his ideas were wrong because the church said they would kill him if he didn't. All of Galileo's books were burned in Italy, but he sent his manuscripts to scientists in other countries. Galileo was the first scientist to base his work on experiments and to find out for himself how nature worked.

These are all examples of what the American Revolution was about. These are the things that started in the hearts and the minds of the people, that they should be able to choose their own government, that they should be able to worship God in their own way, and that they should not be put in jail for their ideas.

I also evaluated the children on the scientific aspects of the project: the design and execution of their experiment, how they recorded and reported on the data, and the conclusion they drew from their results. (I like the approach taken in Figure 4–3!)

I hold all my students to high standards, but I don't expect them all to achieve the same level of understanding. For example, some

FIG. 4-3:   *Galileo-Aristotle*

children were able to retell the lives of the Renaissance personalities in their own words and write coherently about them. They designed experiments to find out if Galileo or Aristotle was correct. However, when I challenged them to think about the relationship between Galileo, Luther, Cromwell, and Leonardo, they had a vague sense that they are related but weren't able to articulate it. And they had very little understanding that these lives had anything to do with the American Revolution. A second group of students were able to see and articulate the relationship between the four biographies, that they all are individuals who stood up to the authority, the system, the conventions of the time. They also had a sense of the relationship between these persons and the American Revolution but had trouble articulating it. The final group enjoyed the stories, saw the connections between the four characters, and also understood how they were the seeds of the American Revolution.

I push all my students to think more deeply and stretch them to demonstrate their understanding, but because of very different levels of development and abilities, I do not expect them all to reach the third stage. What I like about a project like this is that children who do not reach the deepest levels of understanding will still be challenged and actively engaged. They, too, will feel success from the hard work they were able to accomplish. Each level of understanding has its own challenges and fills the children with a sense of accomplishment when they meet them.

CHAPTER FIVE

Why Are Our Shoes Made on the Other Side of the World?

One day a student brought in his collection of baseball cards, and several magazines that reported the value of each card on the traders' market. He had a 1970 Reggie Jackson worth 130 dollars and a Tom Pagnozzi (a relatively unknown modern player) worth five cents. The two cards were made of the same materials and looked nearly identical in style and substance. Why the difference in value? This is the kind of puzzle I love to give my students. It is something that on the one hand may seem obvious but on the other is difficult to explain.

"Because it's older," said Kathy with some certainty. Rather than simply approve or deny the validity of her response, I tried to help her test her hypothesis.

"John, do you have any other old cards?" John pulled out another 1970 card, Bert Campaneris. We found Bert in the price guide— he was valued at only five dollars. "Well, five dollars is more than five cents, so the age of the card may have something to do with its value, but it's not the whole story. What else?"

"Popularity!" another student speculated. "It's worth more because he is more popular."

I asked the children about the most popular player they knew. "Barry Bonds!" they howled. We looked up the price of Barry Bonds: five dollars. So popularity was another factor, but again, not the whole story.

"It must be because he was such a good player," another conjectured. We compared Reggie's statistics to those of Barry Bonds. Bonds had a higher batting average, more home runs, and more runs batted in. No, it couldn't be based on how good the player was.

We continued hypothesizing and testing until they put together the two factors of how many cards there were and how many people wanted them. They discovered the law of supply and demand. When students learn by discovery like this, they are much more likely to understand, remember, and apply their knowledge to other situations. They experience the joy of learning, the satisfaction of tracking down the significant factors and arriving at a conclusion supported by the evidence. They do not need external rewards to motivate them to work.

One measure of true understanding is the ability to apply the principle in a different context. To evaluate their understanding, I asked them to apply the concept of supply and demand in other situations. Why was a diamond so valuable and quartz so inexpensive, for example? They were quick to discern that diamonds were rare and everyone wanted them, quartz was common and not as many people wanted it. When I was sure they all understood the concept, I was ready to end the lesson, satisfied that we had learned something important. Then someone asked, "But Mr. Levy, what about our loom? It is just made of wood and string and yet it cost us four hundred dollars!" Aha! What a great question! It uncovered another factor we had not yet considered: the cost of the labor. Someone took a lot of time to make this loom, and that had to be reflected in its value.

I needed a quick way to illustrate the idea of the cost of labor. I could easily tell them about it, but the challenge is always to give them a chance to discover it themselves. I don't know why the idea came to me; maybe I had read an article in the newspaper about how so many American manufacturing companies were using foreign labor because it was so much cheaper.

"All right, everybody," I said, ignoring the schedule that said we were supposed to begin math, "take off your shoes and tell me where they were made." The children took off their shoes (not without much shrieking and squealing) and began to call out the countries where they were made.

"Korea!"

"China!"

"Taiwan!"

"Thailand!"

Only three out of twenty-three children had shoes made in America. The children were astounded. I was surprised too. When we looked at these countries on the map, it became apparent that not only were our shoes made in other countries, but you couldn't get further away on the earth!

A significant question was beginning to take shape. Why does America, foremost manufacturer on the planet, make so many of its shoes on the other side of the world? That seemed like a pretty grand question. It had a good puzzle in it, implicit dissonance. And if that weren't enough, Massachusetts used to be the shoe-making capital of the world when these students' parents were born. Now hardly a shoe is made here! What happened to shoe manufacturing in Massachusetts?

I was ready to leave these questions for another time and move on to math when Joan said, "Oh, Mr. Levy, I bet it's just our class. If we went to other classes I am sure they would have more shoes made in America." Joan would have fit in with the crowd at Galileo's experiment in Pisa. She would not believe what she saw with her own eyes and looked for another way to explain it. On the other hand, maybe she was right. We needed to be careful about generalizing on the basis of the results of one case.

"How could we find out?" I asked.

"We could do a survey," Joan said hopefully. I saw that this project would involve much more genuine mathematical experience than the lesson I had planned. We quickly identified questions to ask (see Figure 5–1). Then the children wrote letters to all the other teachers in the building asking permission to come in and survey their class. They prepared a schedule, and pairs of students went out over the next several weeks and conducted the surveys. The children also

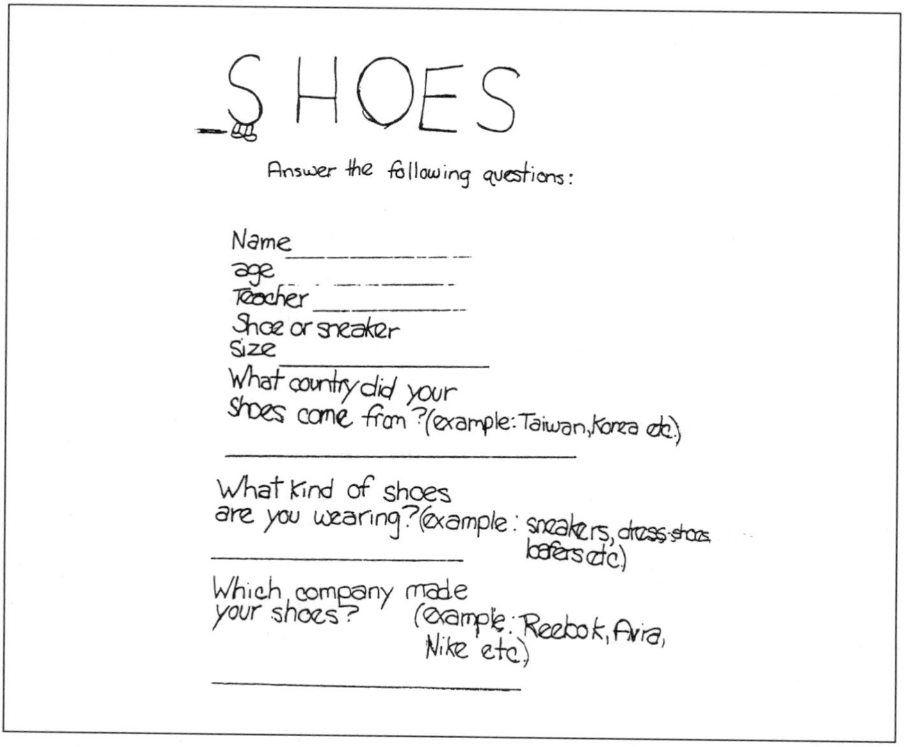

_S HOES

Answer the following questions:

Name _____

age _____

Teacher _____

Shoe or sneaker
Size _____

What country did your
shoes come from? (example: Taiwan, Korea etc.)

_____

What kind of shoes
are you wearing? (example: sneakers, dress shoes
loafers etc.)
_____

Which company made
your shoes?   (example: Reebok, Avia,
Nike etc.)

_____

FIG. 5-1:   *Shoe survey*

surveyed family members and neighbors. Every visitor to Room 9 had to remove his or her shoes and complete a survey. We collected over five hundred forms, at which point I began to wonder what to do next. How do we make sense of five hundred survey forms? I figured this must be what computers are for. I certainly hoped so!

I had never done much work with computers in the classroom, but this seemed a perfect reason to introduce them. A parent of one of the students showed us how to set up a data base, and over the next few weeks the children entered the data from the questionnaires. We were able to generate some interesting questions from this information. For example, Nike made some shoes in Indonesia, some in Korea, and some in the United States. Why would that be? Why did

Dexter still make its shoes in America when so many other shoe companies made their shoes in other countries?

Each child took a different shoe company and wrote them a letter. They included graphs showing the results of our survey.

Life is always more exciting when you are waiting for a letter. For the next month, we greeted every day with eager anticipation. The children would be watching the window with one eye when it came time for the mail truck to roll by. As soon as they saw it, one of the students would go down to the office to help sort the mail and bring back the "prize."

I was impressed that so many shoe companies responded personally to the children's letters (Thom McAn's response is included in Figure 5-2). Only L.A. Gear sent a form letter, and the class decided to boycott its products. Along with the answers to the students' questions, many companies sent trinkets, posters, and bumper stickers. Keds was the most popular shoe in Bowman School, so when Keds wrote back, we also got a huge box that contained Keds sunglasses, Keds key chains with miniature sneakers (made in Korea), and a cross section of a shoe. Most companies also sent slick brochures, which gave us a chance to look briefly at the whole advertising issue. Brenda Sullivan, our art teacher, had the children all design shoes, produce one pair, and create a poster to promote it.

While waiting for responses from the shoe companies, we raised additional questions about shoes. I was curious to see how deep and how broad our shoe study could become, my theory being that you can start with almost anything and through rigorous and imaginative questioning get to the depth and breadth of the world. The children did not disappoint me.

Some students were interested in the history of shoes. When might have been the first time someone had the idea to put something on his feet? How did substance and style change over the years?

Another group explored shoes around the world and how they differed in different countries.

One group was particularly interested in why Massachusetts used to be the center of shoe manufacturing in the world and wasn't

THOM McAN SHOE COMPANY
67 MILLBROOK STREET
BOX 15077
WORCESTER, MASSACHUSETTS 01615-0077
(508)791-3811

February 16, 1990

Miss Pranay Sammeta
c/o Bowman School
Mr. Levy's Class Room 8
9 Phillip Road
Lexington, MA 02173

Miss Sammeta:

I am writing you in response to your survey done recently on the type
of shoes worn at the Bowman School in Lexington, MA. I am very impressed at the work that was done and to what degree your graph
details the breakdown by brand.

To answer your question as to why so many shoes are made overseas,
this is a continuing problem for us. Due to the fact that to make
shoes it is very labor intensive and sometimes requires 150 separate
operations of which all need to be performed by people. There is
very little robotics involved in making shoes as there is more
craft work involved. Just to let you know, we do have one factory
in North Carolina which makes close to 1 million pairs of men's
dress and casual shoes a year.

It was nice for me to see that Balloon shoes were worn by six
people in the school and was equal to other well-known brands such
as Bass, BK and Adidas. I am passing this report along to the
President of Thom McAn to show him how popular our shoes are.
We spend a lot of time and money working with consultants trying
to determine who our customer is and what they think of our shoes.

I think you have done a great job and have done as good a job as the
companies we hire to do similar work.

Thank you for sharing you work with us.

Best Regards,

Jim Miller
Vice President/Merchandise Manager
Athletics/Children's Division

cc: L. McVey

FIG. 5-2: *Letter from Thom McAn Shoe Company*

anymore. I raised the question, What were shoes like in colonial times? because colonial life was a focus of our social studies curriculum. Several children researched this and reported to the class.

Other children were interested in how shoes were made. A number were curious about why particular countries manufactured our shoes. Why Korea, China, and Taiwan, and not India, Germany, or Africa? They did reports on individual countries to try to find out what was happening in those countries that made them suitable for manufacturing shoes.

A final group explored the topic of shoes in literature. They reported on books and stories in which shoes had a starring role.

At the end of a project we always find a way to share what we have done and learned with the community. This helps motivate the children to produce quality work, and gives me an authentic way to assess what they have learned.

For this project we put each group's report together into a book. We then displayed the book along with supporting graphs, charts, letters, articles, and artifacts (a few of the graphs are shown in Figure 5–3). Children from other classes, as well as parents and friends, were invited to come and tour the exhibit.

When other people in the community found out what we were doing, they sent us many interesting articles about shoes and related subjects. These became sources of research and part of our display. Someone even brought us the sneaker (size seventeen!) of Bill Walton, who had just retired from the Boston Celtics.

The children produced many products throughout the project that provided me with opportunities to evaluate their understanding. I also gave a formal assessment, which is shown in Figure 5–4.

This past year, five years since we did this project, I was working on a video and needed a shot of children looking at their shoes to see where they were made. I asked the children to take off their shoes and report their origin while we videotaped the proceedings. I was amazed to find that not only were few shoes made in the United States, few shoes were made in Korea, which was by far the leading manufacturer five years ago! Now the main producer was China, at least in our class. What had happened? Unfortunately, it was the end

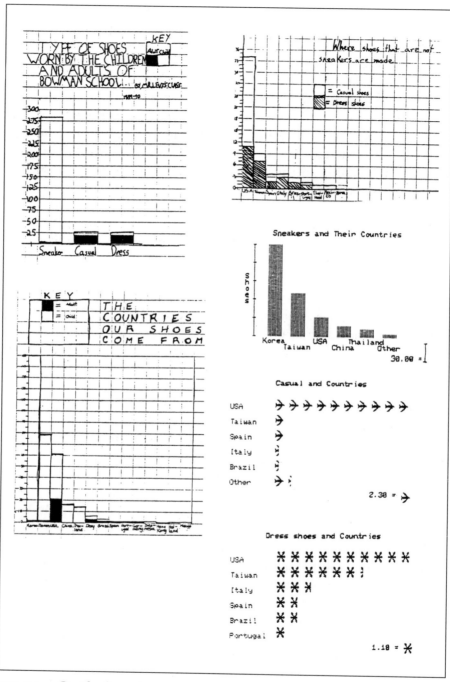

FIG. 5-3: *Graphs from shoe survey*

name_____ date_____

I. SHOE FACTS

1. How many sneakers were worn by children in Bowman School? _____

   How many casual? _____ How many dress? _____

2. How many adults wore shoes made in the USA? _____

3. How many sneakers were made in Thailand? _____

4. How many dress shoes were made in Taiwan? _____

5. How many sneakers were made in Korea? _____

   How many dress shoes? _____ How many casual? _____

6. Which country made the most dress shoes? _____

7. Which country made the most casual shoes? _____

8. Which two countries made the most sneakers? _____

List as many reasons as you can to answer the following
question: "Why does America, foremost manufacturer in the
world. make our shoes in countries half way around the
world?

Answer the following questions in complete sentences. Don't
worry if you can't answer every one. Just do the best you
can.

A. Why do you think some companies still make shoes in
America?

B. Why do you think Korea and Taiwan make our sneakers
rather than England and France? What is special about those
two countries?

C. Why did Boston used to be the shoe making capital of the
world?

D. Why did United Shoe Company go out of business?

E. How did the building of factories in Korea change the
way of life for the people who lived there?

FIG. 5-4: *Formal assessment of shoe project*

of May, so I will have to wait and get next year's class to help me find out.

It was a long journey from a baseball card collection to a book about shoes. But one step naturally followed another. Such is the interweaving of the subjects we study. As we explore the world we find intersections everywhere. I have learned that no matter how far we wander (wonder), we will always find a way back home. Otto Phanstiel, a science teacher from Florida whom I met at the Disney awards, made an extraordinary reference to the periodic table of the elements: When we look across a row horizontally, we are amazed at the unity we find, at how related everything is. When we look down a row vertically, we are amazed at the tremendous diversity. And if we focus on any one element, we are amazed at its absolute and limitless uniqueness.

CHAPTER SIX

What Is the Greatest Number?

Questions are not limited to social studies and science. I use a rather fanciful device to introduce my students to basic geometry. I begin by telling the following story.

My family and I like to take walks together in the woods on Sunday afternoons. Usually we stay together, but there are times when we cannot agree on a direction and split up with a promise to meet again at a designated spot at a certain time.

One Sunday we were walking a familiar trail and I noticed a parting in the brush and weeds alongside the path. It was difficult to tell if it was a real path or just an accidental gap in the ground cover. I wanted to explore further, but my family was not interested, so we separated with an agreement to meet back at the car in an hour.

I followed the quasi-path for about a hundred feet or so up the side of a small hill. The further I went, the more tangled the bushes and weeds became. The path seemed swallowed up by the forest and I was ready to turn around and try to catch up with my family when I heard the sound of voices. They seemed to be in heated debate. I climbed to the top of the hill, looked out carefully from behind the fat trunk of an old oak tree. There, in a hollow surrounded by thick brush, was a circle of twelve characters in animated discussion. As I looked closer, I was shocked to find that the strange characters I saw were the numbers One through Twelve! They were arguing about which number was the greatest and should be crowned king or queen of all the numbers. Number One was speaking first.

"Now what do you think he might have said?" I ask the children.

"I am first, so I should be king!"

"All the other numbers are made from me."

"I am a factor of all numbers."

I like this kind of question because everyone has equal access to it. It is not dependent on prior knowledge. There is a vast array of possible responses, on a variety of levels. Children who don't usually participate often have something to say.

I let the children offer their ideas and then I tell them what I heard.

"I am the greatest," said number One, "because I am the biggest of all numbers." Some of the other numbers snickered, others roared. My students also always express vocal disbelief. "I'll prove it to you," I tell them. "Look at me, you see I have fingers, toes, arms, and legs. I have over two hundred bones in my body and many different organs. Now if you add up all those parts, what do you get? You get *one* me."

The children listen with puzzled interest, wondering what is coming next. "When I look around this room, I see we have twenty-six different people who call themselves *me*. What do we get when we add all those people together? We get *one* class. When I walk down the halls, I see we have many classes here. What do we get when we add up all the classes?"

"A school," the children cry in unison.

"*One* school," I specify. "Now I know that there are many children and their families who go to other schools around here. What do we get if we add up all the people who go to all the schools around here?"

"One town." They are beginning to catch on.

"Very good. Now I know that there are many towns in this region. What do we get when we add up all the towns?"

"One state!" they shout.

"Good. And all the states added together make . . . ?"

"One country!"

"Yes! And the sum of all countries?"

"One world!"

"So now you see, one is really the biggest of all numbers. The sum of everything added together is *one*."

While they are still puzzling over this odd conclusion, I ask, "Now what do you think number One looks like?" I have them all draw a picture of number One. (I like to have the children draw as much as possible. The ability to represent a concept in picture form calls on the most creative aspects of our thinking.)

Their drawings are usually based on the basic form of the numeral 1. They add eyes, hair, arms, and legs in a variety of patterns and styles. The thinking students include only one eye, one hand, one leg, because if the figure is really One, he won't want to have two parts. (Three recent representations are included in Figure 6–1.)

"No," I tell them, "that's not what he looked like at all. You have all drawn variations of the *numeral* 1. But there is a big difference between a numeral and a number. I must show you this difference. A numeral *stands* for a number. It is a symbol that represents a number. It is like the number's name. My name is Mr. Levy." I write my name on the board. "But do I look like that?" I point to the letters of my name. "I mean, what if I walked into class tomorrow and looked

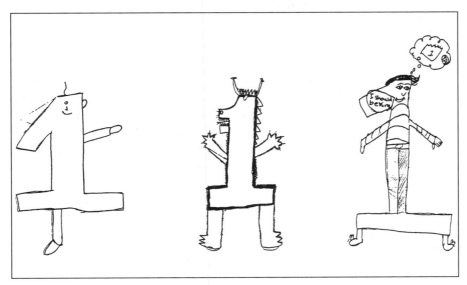

FIG. 6-1:   *Students' ideas of what Number One looked like*

like those letters crawling on the floor? No, the name *Mr. Levy* is a symbol. It stands for me. When you see it, you picture me in your mind. It is the same way with number One. The numeral 1 is the symbol for number One, but it is not what One looks like. Now think of who number One is. Remember his characteristics. The form has to include everything. He must be oneness through and through. What shape do you think this might be?"

I am often surprised how many of them get it. They draw a circle. The circle contains everything within it. It is made with just one line. It is a perfect picture of the whole world. We practice drawing circles, attending to every bump, every dent. I teach them to plan it out before they begin. We draw them with our finger, then with the eraser on our pencils. I teach them to draw very lightly first, so they can make adjustments if there are imperfections in the form. As they see the roundness, they darken it. Making circles is a wonderful way to establish a culture of high expectations. Everyone can try her or his best, and everyone can improve. All the geometric forms based on the other numbers emerge from the circle.

"Now, what color is he?" I ask.

"Blue and green," someone says.

"Why blue and green?" I challenge.

"Because the world is mostly water and earth. Water is blue and earth is green."

"Great idea," I respond. "But do you think number One would want to be *two* colors?" I press them to be true and consistent, even in their imagination, to the concept we are exploring. There are not right or wrong answers in such an imaginative exercise, only more or less thoughtful ones. I push them to support everything they say with appropriate reasoning.

"Any other ideas?"

"I think he should be white, because all the colors mixed together make white," someone offers.

"No," someone else says, "all the colors together make black." I explain the difference between mixing light, which makes white, and mixing pigment, which makes black (actually different shades of brown).

"Excellent thought. He could well be white or black. Any other thoughts?"

"I think he should be all the colors of the rainbow."

"Why is that?"

"Because light is made up of all the colors of the rainbow. He should look like the color wheel."

Earlier in the year we have done some experiments with color, and have studied the color wheel, which is like a rainbow bent into the shape of a circle. "Exactly!" I cheer. "That is, in fact, just what he looked like."

I teach them how to blend the colors together so they cannot tell where the orange stops and the red begins or where the green transforms into blue. We practice over and over. The children learn that I expect the best from them. I stretch them and push them to levels of care and attention they haven't yet known. I expect that same high standard to be applied to everything we do.

I also teach them the geometry of the circle. We learn the vocabulary of *circumference, radius, diameter*. I use the figures they draw for each number to teach the basic forms and vocabulary of geometry.

When I am satisfied that they have worked hard enough on their practice, I give them a piece of high-quality paper. We finish all our work throughout the year on this paper and then bind it together into a book at the end of the year. They get only one piece for each assignment, so they have to plan carefully and fix all their mistakes. It is particularly important to be careful because all the work is done in colored pencil, which does not erase easily. Some errors can be fixed by just going over the error with a stronger stroke or a darker color. Sometimes, if it is a large mistake, it can be turned into an illustration. If all else fails I tell them to draw a single line through the error, and continue. This looks much better than the ugly smudges that often result from trying to erase or cross out errors. We never use opaquing fluid! (Well, hardly ever.)

Their final drawing is the fully colored circle accompanied by a short description of the nature of number One. (It may take us a week to complete the activities associated with number One.)

"Now what do you think number Two said?" I ask.

"I'm better than One because I am twice as big!"

"Stand up and say it like you are really boasting," I push. He does. "Well, that's true, but isn't she setting up number Four, who will clearly beat number Two on the merits of that same argument? What else might number Two say?"

"I should be queen because two heads are better than one!"

"Two is better than One because then you have somebody to play with."

Again, I listen to all their ideas, challenge them to think deeply about what they are saying, to follow the consequences of their logic. There obviously is no right or wrong answer. What counts is their ability to defend their imagination with reason.

I tell them what I heard number Two say.

"Boring! I mean how boring. Can you imagine what the world would be like if everything were just one big same thing?

"We saw before that the whole earth was a picture of oneness. But what happens to the earth as it travels through the heavens? How would life be different if the earth just stood still in space? What changes do we see because it moves?"

"We get night and day!" an astute student responds.

"Right! And what else?"

"We get winter and summer."

"Right! Now what are these, *day* and *night*, *winter* and *summer?*"

"Opposites!" they cry in unison.

"Yes, that's it! And in truth, this is what number Two said. 'I bring some action, some excitement into the boring world of One. I bring the world of opposites.'"

We name all the opposites we can think of, and then I ask what they think number Two looked like. She turns out to be the yin-yang symbol. "What color?" I ask.

"Black and white," someone says.

"Blue and yellow," someone else says.

"Why blue and yellow?" I ask.

"Because blue is a cold color, and yellow is a warm color."

"Absolutely."

"She could also be red and green."

"And why is that?" I prod.

"Because they are opposite each other on the color wheel."

"Wonderful. And what other color pairs are complementary?"

"Blue and orange."

"Right."

"Yellow and purple."

"Right. You can use any of these combinations to make your drawing of number Two."

When number Two is completed, we go on to number Three. We repeat the same procedure, discussing the children's ideas before I tell them what I heard the number say.

Three said, "What a terrible life this would be if we were stuck in the battling world of the opposites. I bring resolution, compromise, synthesis to the conflicts of 'twoness.' Out of the world of black and white, I bring the three primary colors from which all colors are made. Out of man and woman, I bring a child. Out of 'too hot' and 'too cold' I bring 'just right.' I bring something new out of the meeting of the opposites. I bring peace to the warring world of Two."

We look for Three all year. When we recognize classmates arguing in twoness, someone will ask, "Where is number Three?" and we all know what he or she means.

Three looks like a triangle, of course. We draw him inside a circle. All of the geometric shapes we draw come out of the circle. Our circles get better and better as we climb through the numbers. It is a great challenge for the children to divide the circle into three equal parts. We label the points A, B, and C. We practice drawing straight lines. It is amazing how much planning and care need to be exercised in drawing a straight line from A to B. We make all our drawings freehand, so the children will develop an inner sense of the form. We learn about *line segments, angles, vertices,* and the vocabulary of the *polygon.* We bisect each side of the triangle and then connect the midpoints to form a triangle within a triangle. We do this repeatedly until the triangles can't get any smaller.

What color should Three be? The three primary colors, of course, but the colors can be arranged in multitudinous patterns. I teach them shading techniques to make the color darker at the vertices, and then gradually lighten toward the center.

Another wonderful aspect of number Three is that objects need three dimensions to exist in the physical world. I use this opportunity to teach the class about dimensions in space. What does something look like that has only one dimension? What is the name of that dimension? Can we see it? Can we measure it? Something with only one dimension is called a *line*. The name of its dimension is *length*. We can't see it, but we can imagine it. There is a line between your nose and the tip of your outstretched hand. There is a line that goes from the upper right corner of this page to the lower left corner. We can measure it with a ruler in units called *inches, feet, meters*.

Now what happens when we add a second dimension, can we see it? The children quickly hold up a piece of paper. They think it has two dimensions. And it does have length and width, but it also has depth, as thin as it might be. There are instruments that can measure that thinness. Something with two dimensions is called a *plane*. It has length and width, but no depth. We can measure it in squares: *square inches, square feet, square meters*. But how can we imagine something with two dimensions? Where do we find it? Look at the plane that stretches from the floor to the ceiling, front wall to back wall, and divides the room in half. That invisible curtain is a plane.

When a third dimension is added, something can exist in physical space. We can measure it in *cubes*. It is called a *solid*. Everything we see exists in three dimensions. (Although someone is sure to insist there needs to be a fourth: time; if something is not in time it doesn't exist.)

Now is there something that has no dimensions? What would it look like? Start with three dimensions and take away the depth. We are back to a plane. Take away the width and we have a line. What do you have if you take away the length? Something can have no dimensions and yet you can find it right on the page and even show it to someone else. Imagine the midpoint. Or it is a point two centimeters over from the top left corner and six centimeters down. Something that has no dimensions is called a *point*. But I have diverged too far from the point here. Let's get back to the numbers.

Number Four is the number of the earth. We have four directions and four seasons. The Greeks categorized all matter in four elements: earth, water, air, and fire. Four is a number of strength and balance. Where do we see it around us? Look at the construction of our buildings and furniture. Our rooms have (generally) four walls, our tables have four sides, our chairs have four legs. Animals have four legs.

I am not trying to make any mystical claims about these numbers. Rather, I am encouraging my students to look for evidence of how numbers are manifest in our world. We draw a square inside a circle, practicing the techniques we developed with the earlier numbers. They have to think and aim before they draw a line from one point to another. Then traveling around the square counterclockwise, we find a point about an inch past each vertex. When we have four points, we connect them to form a new square inside the first one. Then we traverse the new square counterclockwise and find four new points and connect them. We review all the geometric terms, we practice drawing with care and precision, and then decide which colors Four should be. Any idea that can be defended by reason is welcomed.

Number Five we call the number of the human being. Five fingers, five toes, five senses. I show them the great Renaissance drawing by Leonardo of the man with outstretched arms and legs standing within a circle. If we adjust the arms downward and draw a smaller circle, his head, two hands, and two legs divide it into five equal parts. Then we draw a circle and divide it into five equal parts. (That is a great challenge.) We then connect the points in a five-pointed star, weaving the lines over and under each time they cross (see Figure 6–2).

Six is the first *perfect number*. A perfect number is a number that equals the sum of its factors. The factors of six are one, two, and three. Add the factors together and you get six. Homework that night is to find the next perfect number (twenty-eight). The Six drawing is perhaps the most complicated one we do. We begin with a circle whose diameter is no more than a third of the size of the page. We divide the circle into six parts and mark the point in the center. Then we draw six circles the same size as the first. The center of each will be one of the six dividing points. Each of the new circles will pass

Five is the number of humanbeing

FIG. 6-2: *Freehand drawing of Number Five*

through the center of the original circle and also through the dividing points on either side.

I return to my story: I could not contain my excitement at the idea of the perfect number. I let out a sound of delighted amazement. The numbers heard me, and looked over in my direction. I ran. Besides, it was time for me to go and meet my family.

After this the children have to take the principles we have practiced and apply them to the numbers Seven through Twelve. (Appendix E includes instructions for drawing all the numbers.) We try to discern the genius of each number and where it is manifest in society or the world. Eleven is always the most difficult. (The numeral 11 is the first palindrome. A good homework assignment is, How many times will a digital clock show a palindrome in the course of one full day?)

Leaving the numbers at this point also saves me from having to declare who really was crowned leader of the numbers. The children have to decide for themselves. But no matter how sophisticated the class, they always have one question for me at the end: "Mr. Levy, is that a true story?"

"Yes, my friends. It is a true *story!*"

I usually start this project near the beginning of the year. By covering one number or so each week, we finish all twelve drawings by December. During the process we explore the quality of numbers as well as the quantity. We learn about geometry. We observe the manifestation of number in the world around us. We create metaphors for discussing and solving conflicts. We establish a standard of quality and care that is applied to everything we do throughout the year. We learn the importance of planning and develop techniques in the arts. We practice the process of logic and the exercise of reason in the service of an imaginative inquiry.

In the end we produce a gift for a loved one. Each child puts all of her or his drawings together with grids of the days of each month and produces a beautiful calendar of the shapes of the year. Some lucky relative or friend receives a wonderful present for the holidays.

CHAPTER SEVEN

Poverty of Gratitude

Sometimes my guiding questions come from the particular needs of the community in which I teach. Lexington, Massachusetts, is a suburban town outside of Boston. The poverty here is different from that in urban areas. I call it a poverty of gratitude. I have come to see that if the blessings in life do not awaken a sense of gratitude and compassion, they actually work like a curse. We see it in careless treatment of the environment, insensitive attitudes toward one another, a sense of being owed something by the world. One of my most important teaching responsibilities is to help awaken a sense of gratitude. I want my students to develop the habit of being thankful, to look for opportunities to express thanks. Gratitude preempts complaining. It is a recognition of the Other, which works against the self-centeredness at the root of so many of our social ills.

I first became aware of how much my class needed to practice gratitude when I was invited to teach for a day in Lawrence, an impoverished city with a large immigrant population located on the Merrimack River in northeastern Massachusetts. What could I teach one class in one day that would have any relevance or meaning? I wondered what the students knew about the city in which they lived. I read a little about Lawrence and discovered its interesting origin. In the time of these children's great-grandparents, Lawrence was the woolen-producing capital of the world. Great mills sprang up like dark jewels on the necklace of the mighty Merrimack. Abbot

Lawrence, the town's founder, became wealthy, but the mill workers lived in poverty and worked in squalor. In 1912 they organized against management to improve conditions for the workers. Immigrants from Germany, Italy, and Ireland, usually enemies, united in what became known as the Bread and Roses Strike. Factory workers all over the world might well feel a sense of gratitude for those Lawrence mill girls and laborers who demanded to be treated with some respect and dignity. "Give us bread," they cried, "but give us roses too." Here was something that might give the children of Lawrence a reason to identify with their history and feel proud of their city.

When I arrived in the seventh-grade classroom, I wondered if anything I said would get through to the children. It was a combined bilingual/special education class. The teacher worked hard to get even the slightest amount of attention. The children were much more interested in each other than in any assignment. Several of the boys rose out of their seats periodically to challenge one another. Some girls taunted them, others sat in silence, even when the teacher called on them.

I told them I was from Lexington, and asked how many had heard of my town. Three hands went up out of twenty-six children. I interrupted my lesson plan to teach them a little about Lexington. I told them about the battle there that started the Revolutionary War. Six of them had heard of that. I acted out the British, marching in columns down what is now Massachusetts Avenue. I ran to the other side of the room and played the part of the colonial militia, standing defiantly on the green.

"Disperse, ye rebels!" cried the British general.

"Don't fire unless fired upon" (I had become Minuteman Captain John Parker) "but if they mean to have a war, let it begin here!" I emphasized the few, the proud, the disadvantaged, standing up with principle and conviction against the king. "We are not going to take it anymore. We are standing here for our rights!"

Then I told them about Abbot Lawrence, and how the city of Lawrence had a very different beginning from Lexington's. Lexington was founded by citizens who moved out from the crowded area of Cambridge in search of more farmlands and a better place to raise their families. Lawrence was planned by Mr. Lawrence as a place where he could make money using the power of the mighty Merrimack to drive the mills. I told them how by 1890 Lawrence was the wool-producing capital of the world even though Abbot Lawrence was the one who reaped the riches. I took them up to the strike in 1912 when the mill workers stood up to the managers and owners and they too said, "We are not going to take it anymore. We are standing here for our rights!" We celebrated this sisterhood between our two cities, the little guys uniting and standing up to the big and powerful authorities.

Then I talked about wool. I gave them each a piece of wool and showed them how to twist it. They were amazed to see the fluffy stuff transform into tight yarn. I produced a four-ply strand so strong that the biggest and "baddest" of them could not break it. "Can we keep this?" one child asked.

"Sure," I said, and gave out the rest of the raw wool from the small bag I'd brought.

"Oh thank you!"

"I can't believe we get to keep it."

I had worked with wool in my class in Lexington for several years. Usually when I passed out the raw wool I would hear squeals of "Yich, I'm not going to touch that" or "Hey, no fair! Her piece is bigger than mine." The Lawrence kids were lacking a lot in their lives, but they were rich in gratitude. I saw how much my children needed to learn from the children of Lawrence. I came back to Lexington determined to find ways to make my children aware of and grateful for the blessings they had. An opportunity arose from a most unexpected source.

From Field to Table

A student teacher was presenting a writing lesson. She asked each child to write down the directions for making a peanut butter and jelly sandwich. Then she brought in the ingredients and instructed the children to exchange directions and follow the ones they received to make a sandwich. Peanut butter and jelly have never experienced more bizarre presentations. Within minutes children were spreading peanut butter on their desks, flinging jelly against the wall. When a piece of bread came flying across the room, I lost the little patience I had. "Does anyone know where this loaf of bread comes from!?" I barked in an angry voice.

"Stop and Shop."

"Star Market."

"No, I mean really! Where did it come from?"

"Must be Purity Supreme."

I saw they did not know. "All right," I challenged, "you are going to find out!"

We looked at the wrapper on the bread, and the first ingredient listed was (fortunately) wheat. We got out our atlases and state maps and found where the wheat stalks grew: Kansas. No one in our room knew anybody from Kansas, but we found another teacher who had a good friend there. We wrote to my colleague's friend and asked if she would send us some wheat.

Three weeks later a large, long box from Marti Scott arrived in Room 9. We opened it to find stalks of wheat right off the farm and a plump bag of wheat berries. I held up a golden stalk and said, "Now you are going to figure out how it gets from this stalk to a loaf of bread."

They were eager to begin. They figured out that the first task was to separate the wheat berry from the stalk. They began to pull the small berries off, one by one, and put them in a cup. Each berry is surrounded by a husk with a long "sticky" beard, which had to be removed as well. After about ten minutes the fainthearted were ready to give up. I let them struggle. After thirty, even the most persevering were eyeing the few berries in the cup, looking at how many we had yet to go, and wondering if this was so much fun after all. After several days, they were all begging to return to our regular lessons.

How did they do it on the farm in Kansas? Did the whole family sit around and pick berries off stalks all day? We found some books that showed the huge combines that could separate (*thresh*) an acre of wheat in the time it took us to do a few stalks. Also, since colonial life is a theme of our fourth-grade social studies, we tried to find out how our Pilgrim ancestors did it. A report based on our research is shown in Figure 7–1.

Finally, we invented our own technology. The children tried wrapping the wheat in some sheets and stomping on it to loosen the berries from the stalk. They beat it with sticks. One group put the stalks in a large plastic bag and appointed two brave and trusting souls to hold it against the wall while others took turns chucking a football at it (see photograph).

Whatever method was used resulted in a huge mess. The berries got shaken from the stalk but were left mixed with pieces of stalk, husks, and beards. Again the students plunged into action, rescuing berries out of the morass, collecting them in cups. After twenty minutes of gathering, the children had less than a half-inch of berries in their cups. Once again they searched for ways to make the work

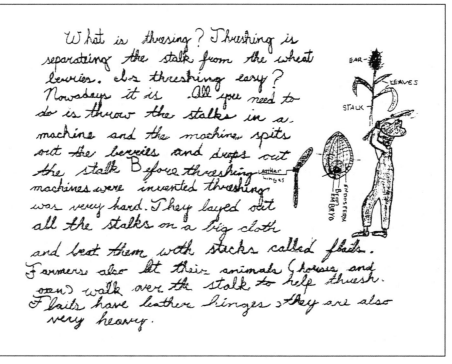

FIG. 7-1: *Threshing description from student's "book work"*

Modern threshing technique

easier. They invented different kinds of sieve and screen arrangements to shake the berries loose. One child invented the tape method— using a piece of masking tape to pick up the chaff and leave the berries behind. A more efficient invention was the water method—if the mixture was placed in a bucket of water, the lighter chaff floated but the heavier berries sank. They just had to scoop the chaff off the top, collect the berries from the bottom, and dry them before they began to sprout. (Of course, some of them set up a sprouting experiment on the side.)

One group tried using static electricity. They rubbed plastic rods with a cloth, and it attracted the husks but left the berries behind. Our most expedient method was discovered quite by accident. One child was holding some of the mix in his hand when he suddenly sneezed. The light chaff blew away and the heavier berries were left in his hand. The wind was our friend; separating the wheat from the chaff by a current of air is called *winnowing*. We went outside on a windy day and brought buckets of the mixture to the top of a climbing structure on the playground and poured it into a large barrel below.

Winnowing the painstaking way

The wind blew the light chaff away and the heavier berries dropped into the barrel. We had the berries separated in a very short time.

Next we had to grind it to produce flour. The students tried smashing it with hammers and crushing it with a rolling pin before I showed them a hand grinder. We took the grinder apart to see how it worked, thus investigating the simple machines that help us do our work. (Simple machines are a fourth-grade science requirement.)

I showed them how water wheels turned the great grinding stones in the old mills. We looked at David Macaulay's *The Mill*. The water wheel turns vertically, but the millstone needs to turn horizontally to grind the grain. When we discovered how to change the direction of the force from vertical to horizontal, we celebrated the gear (see Figure 7–2)!

By supplementing the grain from our own processing with a fifty-pound bag of wheat berries from a health food store, we were able to grind enough flour for each child to make his or her own loaf

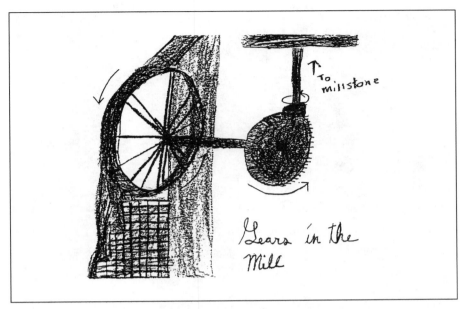

FIG. 7-2:   *How the gear changes vertical rotation to horizontal*

of bread. The children figured out how much of each ingredient we needed to make thirty-two loaves of bread. On the Tuesday before Thanksgiving vacation we baked them. The next day we invited the parents to a performance of music, poetry, and drama. The highlight of the show was a musical we performed that told the story of wheat from planting to baking. At the end of the show we opened a huge cardboard oven and revealed the loaves we had baked the day before. Each child took one home for Thanksgiving.

The next year we decided to plant our own garden of winter wheat. (Winter wheat is planted in September and harvested in June. It will not produce wheat berries unless it is exposed to the freezing elements of winter.) First we read how the Pilgrims cleared the land, and then we took picks and shovels to the ground outside our window.

We discovered some interesting artifacts while digging: toy cars, ancient pens, and brick fragments from the construction of the school. Of less certain authenticity were the fossils and dinosaur teeth

Preparing the soil

some of the children were convinced they had unearthed. Neverthe-less, we put all of these archaeological treasures in our class museum and invited the public to judge for themselves.

When we planted the wheat in September, we learned about designing scientific experiments. We planted four separate plots, each with a different set of constants and variables. One we planted in rows, one we scattered, one we used no manure, and one we used only seeds from our Kansas harvest. Children were out every morning observing and measuring the growth of the small green shoots and recording them in their science logs. One group kept a weather journal and tried to find correlations between the weather and how much the wheat grew. When it did begin to grow, we found our experiments were flawed and that we could draw no conclusions from the different rates of growth we observed because there were too many variables and no control. Did one plot grow faster because it

106

was planted in rows or because it was wheat from the health food store? We try to learn as much from our mistakes as from our successes.

I had the children write about every step of the process. In fact, they were not allowed to proceed to the next step until they had written and illustrated the previous one. Each child made a book describing the entire process from field to table.

The tender wheat stems (about six inches tall) lay dormant over the winter. In the spring they grew rapidly and by May the berries began to appear. We estimated the yield and found the average number of berries per stalk in the four different plots. I also challenged them to figure out a way to count the number of berries in a fifty-pound sack. One child counted out one hundred berries and weighed it on a balance scale. He put enough berries on the other side of the scale to make it balance. Then he knew he had two hundred berries. He put those on one side and balanced it with berries on the other side to get four hundred. Through this doubling technique he soon

The harvest

had a fairly accurate estimate of the number of berries in a whole sack.

At harvest time in June, we reaped the wheat (using scissors, one stalk at a time) and put it in sheaves to dry over the summer. In September these students brought the wheat in to that year's class and challenged them to figure out how it becomes a loaf of bread, passing on the fruit of their labors to the next generation.

The wheat project inspired a lot of good thinking. It demanded much problem solving and a creative imagination. It generated great math opportunities. It covered curriculum in social studies and science. It inspired literary, artistic, and musical activity. But my real goal was to awaken a sense of appreciation for all the work done by many others that makes it possible for us to go to the store and buy a loaf of bread. Recognition is the beginning of gratitude. Now when these children buy a loaf of bread, it won't be something they take for granted.

From Fleece to Fabric

In one of my classes I had a boy who spent twenty minutes every morning in a remedial handwriting session. Michael hated to go. I hated to see him go, because it was always during "good morning" time when we built community by singing and reciting poetry. The handwriting teacher hated working with Michael because his attitude was so bad. Wasn't it ridiculous to persist in doing something everyone hated? Couldn't we find another way to help Michael?

I noticed the handwriting teacher knitting at a faculty meeting. What if she taught Michael to knit? Perhaps the fine motor skills, the rhythmic activity, the concentration, would help his handwriting. Whatever happened, it had to be an improvement.

The teacher was willing to give it a try. I said, "As a matter of fact, my whole class has lousy handwriting. Why don't you come in and teach them all how to knit? That way we wouldn't even be singling him out." The next thing I knew I was standing in front of the class holding a piece of yarn: "Does anybody know where this yarn comes from?"

We found a shepherd and took a field trip to her farm, where we bought a raw fleece for about twenty-six dollars. It was full of straw, dirt, and other unmentionables. We brought it back to class and I challenged the children to figure out how it got from being fleece to being the clothes we wore.

The first step was clearly to clean it. We researched how the Pilgrims did it. They used urine. The uric acid apparently helped prepare the fibers to receive the dye. I am sure this practice was very effective, but we decided not to replicate it. We used a little vinegar and salt instead, and soaked it overnight in a barrel. The next morning the dirty yellow-brown fleece emerged from the water pure white.

Clothes come in many colors, so we read about how the Pilgrims dyed the wool. We experimented with many natural dyes. Bags and

Hanging washed wool to dry

jars with vegetables, flowers, and nuts took up every corner of the room. I bought some samples of bark and bugs (cochineal) that we could not find locally but that promised to produce vibrant color. We had some problems getting the dyes to be permanent. When we washed the wool, the color tended to run out. We read about dyeing, but could not seem to get it right. One of the children lived near a yarn shop. "Maybe someone there knows how to dye the wool and can help us." So we wrote to the yarn shop, and the owner replied with a list of people she thought might be able to help us.

We wrote to some of the people on the list, and Mrs. Duke offered to pay us a visit. She brought pots and materials for dyeing. She showed us how to use copper pipe as a mordant to make the dye stick to the yarn. In fact, Mrs. Duke adopted us, coming back to visit every week, showing us the secrets of the trade, and giving us assignments to carry out for the following week.

Next we had to card the wool. We started with teasel, a thistlelike plant with long spikes used to comb the tangled fibers into long smooth strands ready for spinning into yarn. We celebrated the invention of wooden carders with metal bristles, because the teasel didn't really work too well. I used some grant money to buy a drum carder, which allowed us to produce large quantities of carded wool. The children loved to use it. We enlisted the services of a kindergarten class to help us with the carding.

Now we were ready to spin the wool into yarn. You can produce yarn simply by twisting as you gently pull the fluffy wool apart. It's amazing to see the cloudlike carded wool become so strong that you can't break it. But producing yarn this way takes a long time and is full of frustrations. One of the parents taught us how to make drop spindles that could spin the yarn much more efficiently.

Our drop spindles were made of dowels with a round wooden block attached to the bottom. The combed wool strands, or *roving*, are tied to a string attached to the top of the dowel. The other end of the roving goes over the shoulder of the spinner. With a delicate rhythm of stretching the roving and spinning the wooden block, the fluffy wool is twisted into sturdy yarn. When a full arm's length of yarn has been spun, it is wrapped around the dowel and the process

Spinning on a drop spindle

is repeated. It is as complicated to execute as it is to describe. Many of the students had difficulty, especially the more cerebral ones. Some were only able to master it in pairs, one doing the stretching and the other the spinning.

Michael was a natural at it. The first time he picked up the spindle, he mastered the subtle rhythms. He took great pleasure in winding off huge balls of thickly spun yarn. Other children sought him out for advice and assistance. I don't think anyone had ever asked Michael to help them do something in school before. The smartest kids in the class, who had spent much time washing, dyeing, and carding but were unable to weave anything because they couldn't get any yarn, were lining up to receive Michael's help. All day long

I could see his hands working under the desk. He could do it blind. I never stopped him. He would stand on his desk at the end of the day and ask if anyone had any roving they wanted him to take home. Michael's mom told me that he stopped watching TV and playing Nintendo. All he wanted to do when he got home from school was to spin.

Now it's not that I see a great future for Mike as a spinner. It's just that now that his gift, his genius, had been manifest and recognized by others in the class, he had more confidence to approach areas of difficulty. He applied whatever gifts he did have to the task at hand.

And so we prepared to do our knitting. To heighten our anticipation we made our own knitting needles by sharpening quarter-inch dowels in the pencil sharpener and sanding them to a perfect smoothness. We oiled them for protection and glued a bead on the end. When the needles were completed, I invited all the knitters I knew—parents, grandparents, and other teachers—to come in and teach us how to knit. We had almost one adult for every child, so we were all able to learn in one afternoon. I had a teacher assigned to me as well, because I didn't know how to knit either. (It's important to mention that I didn't know a thing about any of the stuff we were doing. Being a novice offers the great advantage of allowing me to be an example of what it means to be a learner. I get to show my students how to locate resources, what to do when we meet obstacles, how to persevere through difficulties and disappointments.)

Nothing I've ever done before or since did more to transform the social life in my class than learning to knit. There was never a question of what to do when work was finished. The children wanted to stay in and knit every recess; when the weather was nice they took their knitting outside. It showed me how starved our children, girls *and* boys, are to make beautiful things with their hands. But the most

Knitting during recess

amazing thing was their conversations. Boys and girls together, sitting in clumps around the room, talking peacefully, calmly about every imaginable subject. I learned more from listening to their conversations than any tests could ever reveal.

Everyone was required to knit a twelve-inch square. Some children did much more. Many knit stuffed animals, scarves, and clothes for their dolls. Tommy knit covers for his most valuable baseball cards.

Mrs. Duke also showed us how to warp the loom, and we learned to weave the yarn we had washed, carded, dyed, and spun. Each child made a beautiful wall hanging that they took home with great pride.

Day after day Leanne brought in bags of white hair from home. It turned out to be from her dog. She was able to spin the dog hair into yarn on the drop spindles, and weave a beautiful blanket for her dog out of the dog's own hair!

The last step in all our projects is to share what we've learned with the community. We set up a wool museum and invited other classes and parents to see all the stages between the raw wool and the finished product. Small groups of children became the experts at each station.

One group prepared an introduction. They did some research on wool and found it had some amazing, seemingly contradictory, properties. It can be worn in the coldest climates to keep people warm, but it is also worn by the Bedouins in the deserts of Egypt to keep cool. It is so strong that the ancient Greeks used it to make armor, and the Mongolians, to build their houses (yurts). (Wool achieved this great strength when it was felted.) But it is also so soft that it is used to make babies' blankets. It is fire resistant, so firemen carry wool blankets in their trucks and use them to wrap around a person whose clothes are on fire. But it is also water resistant. Fishermen's wives knit their husband's sweaters without washing out the lanolin, and the sweaters keep out the sea water. Wool is also incredibly resilient; the fibers bounce back to their original shape when wrinkled. (That is why our suits are made from wool, it resists wrinkling.) For this same reason it is wrapped inside the covers of major league baseballs.

They also found out that wool had a fascinating history. The Medicis built their wealth on the wool trade in Renaissance Italy. England's major trade staple was wool. George Washington raised sheep and encouraged all patriots to do the same so America wouldn't be dependent on England for cloth. The Australian economy was built on wool. Shepherds in Spain were executed for selling the prized Merino sheep out of the country.

Another group was interested in why it was that wool had all these amazing and seemingly contradictory qualities. They studied various fibers under the microscope (see Figure 7–3): wool, linen, cotton, and silk; hair from camels, rabbits, goats, and sheep. They designed a chart illustrating all the fibers, and they explained how the structure of the wool accounted for its extraordinary properties. These children developed a great disdain for polyester, which looked like a worm under the microscope. Wool was thick, with scales. It had an inner core and an outer scaly wall. Polyester had no complexities of structure or texture.

At the introductory station visitors received a small piece of raw

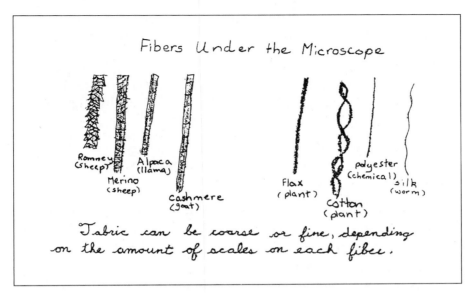

FIG. 7-3: *Fibers under a microscope*

wool and took it to the second station, where that group showed them how to wash it. Then they went on to the dyeing experts who showed them our dye chart and let them dip their wool into one of the dyes. The next position was the carders, then the spinners, then the weavers and knitters.

The final station was a display of all the work the children had completed. The highlight was a scarf that stretched all the way across the ceiling and then some, measuring thirty-three feet. It had been knitted by Tuuka, a student who had just moved to America from Finland. He was tall, blond, very quiet, and extremely shy in class. He spoke no English when he arrived. The work with the wool was great for Tuuka. He was able to participate in all the hands-on activities, including writing and illustrating his book. He was able to endure our class discussions without going crazy because he would always be knitting. He picked up the language very quickly, and I am sure his knitting in class had something to do with it. It also served as his entry into the social fabric of the class. As his scarf grew longer and longer, we had an excellent opportunity to practice our math skills. Every night we had homework about Tuuka's scarf: Tuuka knits six rows to make an inch of cloth. If he knits . . . ; or, It takes Tuuka twelve minutes to knit three rows. If he knits for an hour . . .

We covered many aspects of our fourth-grade curriculum through this project. We wrote and illustrated every step of the way. We experimented with dyes. We read about wool and researched its history and properties. We studied its structure under the microscope and saw how its design related to its exceptional properties. Perhaps most important, we followed a process through from beginning to end, and became aware of the enormous amount of work it takes to produce the clothes we wear, even though the entire process is mechanized today. These students have a unique appreciation, born of their own sweat and labor, for the machines that replaced the human labor of the Pilgrims. They probably also have an appreciation for what was lost when we moved from an agrarian to an industrial society.

Did it affect their handwriting? Well, by the end of the year everyone's handwriting was better. Was it because of the knitting? That will have to be the subject of another experiment.

CHAPTER EIGHT

How Did Our Town Get Its Name?

Some questions arise in the course of traditional curriculum. A book about the history of our town, Lexington, claimed that no one knows where the name Lexington came from. I couldn't resist. Why don't we know where the name Lexington came from? After all, we pride ourselves on our rich history. How could we not know the origin of our name?

This was a great question, but I didn't know where to go with it. I never know when a question will take root and flower into a comprehensive investigation. Usually it's when a child has an idea I would never have thought of. So I was delighted when Sasha offered, "Mr. Levy, I have an aunt who lives in Lexington, Kentucky. Maybe they know down there." Someone else had heard of a Lexington in Texas, so we began to wonder how many Lexingtons there were in the United States. We went to the library and looked for Lexingtons in atlases, on state maps, on road maps, in geographic indexes, in dictionaries, and in encyclopedias.

We found references to twenty-four Lexingtons in the United States. This was particularly significant because no single source we found had listed more than sixteen! The children were thrilled to know more than *National Geographic* about the Lexingtons in our country. Since there were twenty-four kids in our class, this seemed like a project destined to happen.

I am always looking for opportunities to help my children develop the art of asking their own questions. Often when visitors come to the room, I get them to agree to answer a few of the children's questions. Each table of students is then allowed to choose one question that they think will reveal the genius of our guest. Asking questions is one of the most important skills to practice in our schools. I incorporate the asking of questions into every project we do.

In this case, we had to think of what questions to ask the other Lexingtons. How did you get your name? was the most essential, but the children quickly expanded into other areas. Did any famous events ever happen in your town? Did any famous people come from your town? What do people do there for a living? What do they do for fun? Have any weird things happened in your town?

We decided to address our letters to the mayor, figuring there had to be someone in charge, and got the towns' zip codes from the *Zip Code Directory* (which listed only twenty-one Lexingtons—I suppose three were too small to have their own post office). Each child then wrote a letter with his or her own questions attached.

Our first response came from Lexington, Georgia, which claimed to be the smallest Lexington—population, 276. The mayor sent pictures of the town, his own house among them, along with a letter describing the town's history. Farmers who had ruined their land planting tobacco in Virginia and North Carolina had migrated to Georgia and founded Lexington in 1806. There were a lot of interesting issues to explore around that. They took the name of Lexington, as did many other southern cities in the early 1800s. That raised another interesting question: What was the spirit they were trying to represent in choosing the name Lexington?

Each Lexington opened a window into a different aspect of our country's history and geography. We learned about the pioneers who traveled westward in search of new land, gold, freedom, or adventure. Lexington, Oklahoma, was the first town incorporated in Oklahoma. Its residents sneaked out the night before the appointed time to claim homestead property. We learned about the Oregon Trail through the story of Lexington, Oregon. The great railroads gave birth to Lexington, Nebraska, whose citizens changed the town's name from Plum Creek to Lexington in 1889 because Plum Creek did not sound important enough for the great city they planned to become when the Union Pacific routed the railroad through their town. To our surprise, there were two Lexingtons in Ohio. One was founded by Quakers from Virginia because they did not want to be in a state that had slaves. They chose the name Lexington because it was a symbol of freedom. The other Lexington in Ohio and the Lexington in New York were founded by soldiers who had fought in the Revolutionary War.

Each child wrote a story describing how his or her Lexington got its name. Three of these student stories are presented below:

Lexington, Michigan

At first Lexington was called Green Bush. In 1846 Reuben Diamond changed the name to Lexington because his wife's cousin was Ethan Allen. The latter was inspired by the Battle of Lexington in the Revolutionary War.

Green Bush was the first settlement on the shore of Lake Huron north of Point Huron.

In the early days of Green Bush, shingles were used as currency. The price was one thousand per dollar. Ten thousand bought a barrel of flour, while twenty thousand bought a barrel of pork.

In 1846, as we have seen, the name was changed to Lexington. In 1855 Lexington was incorporated. John Divine was the first president.

For a town this size, Lexington has a surprising importance in Sanilac County. The churches, cemeteries, and library are there. As of 1986, Lexington had a population of 765. The main industries are Aunt Jane brand pickles and Pioneer brand sugar.

Lexington, Texas

Lexington is a small town in Lee County which is in southeast central Texas. It was founded by James Shaw in the fall of 1837. He received the land as an award for fighting in the battle that freed Texas from Mexico.

In 1850, Shaw, Sam Riggs and others met for the purpose of naming the town. After much discussion on the subject of names, Mr. Gray said that Lexington would be a good name. He thought of that name because of the battle fought on the green of Lexington, Massachusetts.

Lexington, Texas's population is 1,600. There are lots of rolling hills and cattle ranches in the community. There is also a market for livestock. There is oil, gas, and coal in the ground of the Lexington area.

Lexington, Ohio

Lexington, Ohio, was founded in 1805–06 by Quakers from Virginia. They came to Ohio because they didn't want to be in a state that had slaves. They chose the name of Lexington as a symbol of freedom.

Today, they are proud of their fire engines.

Some Lexingtons claimed unique distinctions. Chewing gum was invented in Lexington, Indiana. Lexington, North Carolina, is the self-proclaimed Barbecue Capital of the World. A town restaurant catered dinners at the White House for President Jimmy Carter. Lexington, Illinois, has a blacksmith plant (one of only three in the United States) that ships horseshoes all over the world. Above all, we learned what the spirit of our own town represented to the rest of the nation.

The information we got from the different Lexingtons was astounding. There were letters, photographs, pamphlets, even books. Some Lexingtons sent artifacts—stickers, ashtrays, pencils, and letter openers—bearing their name. The information was spectacular but overwhelming. The last part of any project we do is to share it with the community, but this seemed too big. There was too much stuff to display, and we did not know how to exhibit it. I asked the children, Who knows how to make displays? Where do you see displays that teach you about something?

Museums! they cried. So we wrote to the Museum of Our National Heritage here in Lexington, explaining what we had collected and asking if someone from the museum would like to come over and take a look. Maybe they could help us figure out a way to display our project. Two people came from the museum and were very impressed at what the children had collected. They invited us to the museum and took us into the cavernous basement where they put their exhibits together. We met with the curator and the designer, and they showed us how they go about designing an exhibit. They let the children practice with stuff they had lying around, and eventually we came up with a structural design. The children were each given one large piece of foam core to organize and display all the information they had received from their Lexington. The museum director said that if our display was good enough, they would show it at the museum.

Now that we knew we would be producing a display, we wrote a second letter to each Lexington, explaining how fascinated we were by the information sent and asking for any additional artifacts that would make the exhibit more vivid. We soon began receiving packages and boxes. The children came to school every day with tremendous enthusiasm and anticipation. When a box arrived, we would stop everything and open it together. The excitement generated from the earlier responses was now multiplied tenfold. Lexington, Texas, sent a big burlap bag of peanuts that were grown in Lexington, a police badge, and a banner sporting their high school team's name, the Lexington Eagles (see photograph).

We learned about the beet sugar industry from Lexington, Michigan, whose mayor sent examples of the stages in producing sugar, from raw beets to refined powder. He also sent some pickles, another big industry there. We got a horseshoe and a giant beer nut mug from Lexington, Illinois. Many more photos and books arrived, along with copies of historical documents like the original certificate of the founding of the town.

Local newspapers covered the project here, but we were even more excited to receive copies of newspapers in Georgia and Missouri that described our project to the people who lived there. (The Lexington, Georgia, article is included as Figure 8–1.)

Several Lexingtons did not respond to the first letter, but the second letter explaining our exhibit encouraged them to participate. Even after the second letter, two Lexingtons did not respond. So one day I sent the two children who had written to the mayors of these

Lexington, Texas

towns to the office to look up the area code of their Lexington, and we called information and asked for the number of the mayor or the town hall or wherever we might speak to whoever was in charge. The children called and explained how the project was going and how much we needed to have their Lexington represented. "Oh yes, the letter is right here on my desk. We were planning to get to it soon. We'll do it right away." Some of our best artifacts came from these tardy respondents. In the end, we had one hundred percent participation, and the children learned an important lesson in perseverance. If these two towns hadn't responded after the phone call, we might have had to pay them a personal visit! You do whatever it takes to get the job done.

The Oglethorpe Echo, Thursday, May 18, 1989

Mayor Doug Clark picks out Lexington, Mass. from courthouse sign.

A Lexington, Mass. fourth graders exhibit on Lexington, Ga.

Lexington, U.S.A. is project of Massachusetts fourth graders

Over the winter months Mayor Douglas Clark has been corresponding with Eric Rosenbaum of Lexington, Massachusetts. He has been helping the fourth grader complete his portion of a historical research project on which his class at Bowman Elementary School was working.

The class wrote to 20 of the 23 Lexingtons in the country. Three of the Lexingtons had no zip codes and so the students were unable to contact them. It started as a project to track down the roots of their town's name. But they discovered that of the 20 towns they were able to contact, all were named, directly or indirectly, for their town.

There are Lexingtons as far south as Texas, as far west as Oregon and as far north as Massachusetts and New York. Each child in the class wrote to the Mayor of a Lexington, not only asking how their town received its name, but also asking questions about the towns' past as well as its current status. They received postcards and collateral material from which they were able to construct a large display.

They found that Lexington, Georgia, may be the smallest Lexington in the country. Settled in 1790 by farmers from Virginia and incorporated in 1806, its name was chosen in honor of the Revolutionary War town of Lexington, Mass.

Lexington, Oregon, is only slightly larger: It was founded in 1859 by Wm. Peneld, whose wife, Jane, wanted the town named for her birthplace, Lexington, Ky.

Lexington, Ky., is the largest Lexington. Legally founded in 1775, it too was named after "the small Massachusetts town that played such a large role in the American Revolution."

Chewing gum was invented in Lexington, Indiana. Lexington, N.C., is called "The Barbecue Capitol of the World," though it is primarily noted for its furniture.

The student's exhibit was on display at the Visitors Center on Patriots Day, a celebration in Massachusetts of the Battle of Lexington Green which started the Revolutionary War. It included photographs of Lexington, Ga., and several letters on official town stationary. There were pictures of the county courthouse as well as several residences. Also one of Mayor Clark beside the sign outside the courthouse with the distances to other Lexingtons.

The students decided that since there were only towns named for theirs in the USA, the roots for their town's name must be in England. There are two possible explanations for the Lexington, Mass., name. Sir Robert Sutton had the title Lord Lexington when the Massachusetts town was incorporating, Lord Lexington was related to the Governor of the precinct, Joseph Dudley. It may well have been named for Lord Robert Lexington. The other theory is that the town may have been named for Laxton, a town which no longer exists in England. As Lexington means "town of Lexton," it may be that, through careless spelling or unclear penmanship, Laxton became Lexton, and then Lexington.

It is from those same roots that Lexington, Georgia, draws its name.

FIG. 8-1: *Article in* Oglethorpe Echo *(Georgia) describes our project*

Along with the panel each child prepared for his or her Lexington, we worked on several class panels, including a hand-drawn map of the United States with pins to show the locations of all the Lexingtons (see photograph) and a collage of the letterheads of all the different Lexingtons. We also painted "The Lexington Family Tree" showing the branches of all the Lexingtons rising from the base according to the dates of their founding. It turned out they were all named after us or after another Lexington that was named after us. Our Lexington had children and grandchildren Lexingtons all over the country!

The museum was proud to display our exhibit that spring. We sent a letter to each Lexington telling about the final display, with a description of what we wrote about their town and a photograph of the exhibit. We also told them they could ask to display the exhibit in their town and promised we would make it portable for travel.

21 Lexingtons with zip codes in the United States

Exhibit at Museum of Our National Heritage

As the year came to an end we turned our attention to England. There was no Lexington in England, but we found one reference to a Laxington in the eleventh century. There are three Laxtons in England today, and the British Consulate told us that it was likely they were abbreviations of Laxington. We wrote to officials in each town, and although none of them could trace any direct relation to our town, one of them told us about an Angle or Saxon chieftain from the time before the Norman conquest named Laexa. If Laexa's people had settled the town, it might have been called Laexingtun, meaning Laexa's town. Using all we knew about historical evidence and methodology, we felt justified in concluding that our town might well trace its origin to this barbarian chief across an ocean and a millennium. Who would have guessed?

CHAPTER NINE

What Is the Biggest Change in Your Town Since You Were Born?

Germinating an Idea

One summer afternoon I was jogging down the newly constructed bike path in Lexington, eyeing the tall, swaying, pale green stalks of full-grown rye that were growing alongside. My class plants a small plot of wheat outside our classroom every year. We harvest each stalk with great ceremony and treat every berry as a gift-wrapped treasure from the earth. I wondered how my students would react when they rode their bikes by the bountiful rye, ripe for harvesting, stretching for several miles along the side of the path. Would they rejoice in the familiarity of the grain? Or in the midst of such plenty would they think I had misled them about the precious value of every berry? Who planted that rye, anyway?

A little further down the path I saw a hand-painted sign whose rude, uneven letters beckoned hot and weary bikers, joggers, and skaters. "Cold Drinks and Refreshments!" It was the rear of the Italian restaurant whose prominent, professional sign in front along Massachusetts Avenue was a town landmark. I wondered if the crude, hand-made sign attracted the people who used the path. Had business increased? Did front-door customers sit at tables next to sweaty bikers? Did Rollerbladers have to take off their skates before entering?

In the short time I was on the path I saw walkers, bikers, Rollerbladers, baby carriages, dog walkers, and other joggers. I wondered how well all these different users coexisted. I remembered a recent article in the local newspaper about a cyclist who had pinned down the feet of an elderly woman with the front tire of his bike, grabbed her by the throat, and shouted in her face. The dog she was walking on a leash had strayed into his path. He had nearly crashed trying to avoid it. Who has the right of way on the path? Who decides? How do adults settle their differences?

On the way back home I saw several abutters in their backyards. I wondered how they felt about the tremendous popularity of the path. Did they enjoy watching the parade, or were they annoyed at the invasion of their privacy?

Little did I realize at the time that I was planning my curriculum for the next school year. But in the angst of August, my bike path wonderings came back to mind. The effect of the bike path on our town seemed a topic rich with opportunities for exploration and learning. It was especially relevant to my students as a safe link between East Lexington, where they lived, to the center of town, where the action was. Families often rode the entire eleven-mile, four-town stretch.

I imagined interesting math activities such as graphing the number of uses and the volume of traffic. My fourth-grade science curriculum included a study of simple machines. The bicycle is a perfect example of simple machines in action. The land had a rich history before the bike path. I remembered years ago when they dug up the railroad tracks. What happened to the railroad? Why did it go out of business? Researching how the land was originally used would lead into my social studies curriculum of colonial life and local history. Perhaps we could write a book about our findings.

But how could I get my students to come up with the bike path topic on their own, to create their own questions, pursue the answers, and finally share what they found with our community? I put my plans on the shelf and came into class with one question: What is the biggest change that has happened in your town since you were born?

At first the children suggested things like: we put an addition on our house; my little sister was born. They hadn't grasped what it meant to affect the whole town. It is easy to take for granted that our students understand what we are talking about. Much of teaching is getting underneath our assumptions and making concepts explicit. Once we understood the concept of affecting the whole town, one child leaped out of his seat and cried, "The bike path!"

I was delighted (and relieved—even though I couldn't think of any other big changes in our town in the last nine years). I asked the question because I think it is important for the children to feel that the topic of our study comes from the natural activity of our class. It does not matter whether the topic really comes from the children or whether I engineer the experience so that they feel like it does. Either way, they have a stake in the project that they otherwise would not have. They are motivated. They feel like explorers, charting new ground. Most of all, they see that learning does not begin with a textbook or workbook but rather with observing the world and asking questions about it. If they had come up with a better answer than the bike path, I would have followed it.

Plotting Our Course

Once we had established the bike path as our subject, it was natural to consider how it came to be. Last year there was not a bike path. This year there was. What happened? We raised numerous questions to guide the course of our study. The children raised most of the questions, but as a member of the learning community, I added my questions to the board too, some that stemmed from my own genuine interest, others that I thought would lead us into areas of prescribed curriculum. For example, I have to teach about life during colonial times, so I needed to make sure that there were some questions that would lead us to study the way people lived on the land before it was a bike path. Does anyone remember what the path was like before it became a bike path? Several children remembered the railroad. And before the railroad? No one knew. So one of our questions became, What was the land used for before it became a railroad? I knew this would get us back to life in colonial times.

After we had filled the board with questions, we organized them according to categories. This helped us get to the heart of the questions. Duplicates were weeded out. Vague questions were refined.

Related questions were combined. In the end, we identified ten distinct areas of interest.

One set of questions had to do with planning. The path ran through four different towns. How did four towns get together and plan the construction of the path? What issues had to be considered? Another set had to do with the history of the land. Some questions had to do with the effect of the path on the abutters, others with its effect on business. Several questions dealt with its impact on the environment.

Some questions concerned issues of safety, while others focused on how the people using the path in different ways cooperated. Some of the questions were about how a bike path is constructed. What is blacktop anyway? Some were about the bicycle. When was it invented? How did it change over the years? Finally, how much had the bike path cost, and who paid for it? (For a more complete list of questions generated, see Appendix F.)

Since we had so many categories of questions I asked each student to write down the names of her or his first three choices. This way, they could work in areas of interest, and I would still have some control over the makeup of the groups. There were twenty-six children in the class, so I assigned two or three children to each group. Their challenge was to research their topic and put the information they discovered in a form that could be shared with others. I mentioned the possibility of writing a book if we found out enough interesting stuff.

Off We Go

Each group's first task was to look over the questions in the category, refine them, expand them, and write each one on a large note card. Any information discovered relating to that question could then be put on the note card. I asked each group to imagine where they might find the information they needed. Some groups, like the history group or the bike group, might find written materials in the library. But other groups would have to locate and consult local residents. I knew that there was a committee in town called Friends of the Bikeway. A brochure about the bikeway listed members of the committee, and we wrote to them first, asking for names of people who might be able to help us in specific areas. We also asked the committee members if they were aware of aspects of the bike path that would be interesting for us to study.

From the list of names we received, we made further contacts and began inviting people to come into our class and address us about particular issues. We had the planning directors of Lexington and Arlington speak to us about the planning process. The Lexington town engineer came in to speak about costs and construction. A selectman spoke to us about the politics of planning.

We were also visited by a bicycle enthusiast who told us about the history of the bicycle and about the scientific and technological advances over the years. A railroad historian described the activity of the railroads and their eventual local demise. Policemen who

Mr. Sawyer demonstrates the "penny farthing"

patrolled the path on bicycles came in and told us about safety rules and crime on the bike path.

The group researching the effect of the bike path on the abutters made several trips to town hall, where the assessor showed them how to read the maps and identify the properties that abutted the bike path. The safety group visited the police station and got to look at the computer and print out all the reports that had been filed relating to incidents on the bike path, which ranged from vandalism to suicide. The children studying the effects of the bike path on business went into town and interviewed the shopkeepers. The group investigating the different uses of the path spent several weekends interviewing people on the path and published a survey in the local newspaper. (Whenever a group left school property, they were accompanied by two adults, usually a parent and a tutor.)

One of the great things about this project was the way the walls between school and community crumbled. The children were very engaged because they felt the community was interested in what they were doing. They worked with the highest standards because they knew many adults were waiting to see the results.

Digging Up the Past

When you open up the doors of your classroom to the community, you never know who may come in. We were visited by one elderly gentleman who had read a survey in the local newspaper written by the group studying the effects of the path on the abutters. He was moved to come in and tell his story in person. He told us that the construction workers who built the path had knocked down his fence and refused to put it back up. He was still bitter. The children were sympathetic to his plight and promised to look into the matter through their "connections." They wrote to the Friends of the Bikeway Committee and the town engineer about the situation.

Meanwhile, we were visited by Mrs. Eddison, a selectman for the Town of Lexington. Her late husband, Jack, had been instrumental in pushing the project during the early planning stages. The path in

131

Lexington is named for him. Mrs. Eddison brought in some of her husband's files, a gold mine of information. The most significant folder contained notes from a public meeting held in 1985 in which opinions about building the bikeway were solicited by the Board of Selectmen. We combed through the notes and found over fifty re-corded comments, both positive and negative. Concerns included litter, vandalism, crime, safety, cost, and maintenance. Several people objected to building the bike path on political grounds, claiming that transportation money (the project was being funded by money from the Department of Transportation) should not be used to support a project that was primarily recreational. One person argued the liber-tarian position that public funds should not be used for causes that are used by only a small portion of the citizens: a bike path should be paid for by the people who use it, not the taxpayers.

These opinions provoked lively discussion. They also proved to be an important source of research. If we could establish that the early fears were unfounded, this would be very valuable information for other towns who were planning to construct a bike path. Indeed, we had received letters from the planning departments of the towns of Concord and Burlington, both of whom had read about our project in an article that appeared in the newspaper and who requested the results of our research for their own planning process.

Fortunately, Mr. Eddison had written the names of the speakers by each entry. We looked up the addresses of the people and wrote to them to see if their fears and concerns had been justified or eradicated now that the path was built.

One of the names that appeared on the list from the 1985 meeting was the man who had come in to tell us his story of the destroyed fence! He had spoken vociferously against the path at the meeting, fearing that unsavory elements from urban areas would use the path to rob people in our town. When the town engineer responded to our letter asking why the man's fence had not been rebuilt, we found out the fence had been built on property owned by the state; the city had offered to rebuild the fence on the man's own land, but he had refused. It was very interesting to see the opinion of the class change from sympathy for the man to indignation at his unreasonable fears and demands. This was an important lesson in hearing all sides before making a judgment.

A Lesson in Courtesy

One of the people who spoke at the 1985 meeting was a woman we'll call Nancy Jones. She was opposed to the building of the path. Claire wrote to her asking if her opinion had changed any since the path was built. Mrs. Jones wrote a nice letter back to Claire, explaining that her opinion had not changed and that she still did not think it was an appropriate use of public funds. She also wrote a letter to me:

Dear Mr. Levy:

Recently I received a letter from one of your students, Claire Stevens, asking me to answer a couple of questions about the bicycle path, and I was happy to respond.

However, Mr. Levy, I was displeased at how the letter was addressed. The envelope read "Nancy Jones." It would seem to me that this is hardly the proper way to address an envelope and certainly an inappropriate way to address an older, married person. The letter's salutation read, "Dear Nancy Jones." Is this the way a fourth grade pupil should address me? It is very sad that young people have no concept of "proper" letter writing/envelope addressing. Quite frankly, I consider this just a matter of common courtesy, which also seems to be missing in grade school education.

Sincerely,
Mrs. Nancy Jones
cc: Kay Dillmore, Principal
    Lois Coit, Chairman, Lexington School Committee

My students were very irritated. Who did she think she was, anyway? They were upset by the tone of the letter, by the unreasonableness of her expectation, and by the fact that she seemed to judge the whole school system by this one incident. Most offensive to the children was the fact that she had sent copies of the letter to our principal and to the chairwoman of the school committee. "Why couldn't she just tell us?"

But in the midst of their outrage, I gave them a challenge. Here was obviously a woman who was displeased with the school system and with the general state of youth in our times. "When you're finished with Mrs. Jones," I challenged them, "I want her faith in the children of today to be restored, and her opinion of the schools in Lexington to be transformed." Secretly, I quite agreed with Mrs. Jones on the point of courtesy. Any increased awareness of its importance would be well worth the effort and time we might appropriate to the cause.

Several children wrote letters to Mrs. Jones (see Figure 9–1 for one example). A variety of feelings were expressed, but all in a polite and friendly manner. We wrote her and invited her to come in and visit. I trusted that her presentation on behalf of courtesy would have a much greater effect on the children than my exhortations would. I was thrilled a week later to get a call from Mrs. Jones agreeing to come and visit.

The children were not so thrilled. In fact, they were petrified. The moment before her arrival children huddled in fear, some hiding under their desks, one literally in tears. A tall, sharply dressed woman walked in and took a seat in front of the class. Her short white hair was stylish and neatly combed. The children sat stiffly in their seats, ready to be excoriated for their inconsiderate abuse. Mrs. Jones spoke in a precise, businesslike tone. "I run a business. If I get a job application that has a mistake in it, that letter goes right into the circular file." I was amazed. She was not an old crotchety biddy as we had prejudged. She was coming from a place of business! Her concern was that things need to be done right in the business world.

"But we didn't know how you wanted to be addressed," one child protested.

"We just saw your name on some old notes from a meeting."

"Some women are offended if you call them Mrs., they like to be called Ms."

"How were we to know?"

Bowman School
9 Philip R.D.
Lexington M.A
02173
Room 9
March 23, 1994

Dear Mrs. Jones,

We have read your letter aloud in class and it has brought up a big issue. We have sent many letters to different people and not yet gotten a response quite like yours. We have been discussing this matter in class, and some people have some disagreements. We are a different generation than yours and we have been taught different things. We think that common courtesy is an important thing to be taught because as we write more and more letters to different people, the more we might need it. Some people think it might not be needed because it isn't what we are usually taught in education these days. Some people think it's not needed because they don't know much about it. But we would be interested if you could come in and tell us a little more about it and change some of our minds. It has brought up a large issue and we would like to discuss it

Sincerely
Tommy

FIG. 9-1: *Letter to Mrs. Jones*

"In the business world," Mrs. Jones explained, "if I have to write someone and I do not know the proper title or spelling, I make a phone call to find out before I send the letter. You have to do it right." This really was courtesy: to spend the extra time it takes to do it right, all out of an impulse to honor the importance of the other.

Mrs. Jones had indeed become our friend. The children saw her point, and many agreed that courtesy was a virtue worth striving for. Mrs. Jones made a big impression on us, and I think we left a good one on her as well.

Bringing in Math

This project offered many opportunities to cover required curriculum. We integrated math by collecting data on how and how often the path was used. (Figure 9–2 is a form we used.) The Friends of the Bikeway Committee needed to count bicycle traffic for the state records. They wrote us and asked if we could help out. Someone from the state Department of Transportation gave us the results of the counts they had conducted in 1980, 1985, and 1990 of bicycles along Massachusetts Avenue, a major road that runs parallel to the bike path. We spent several afternoons after school and several weekends counting traffic on the path. We also recorded the different kinds of activity on the path, including bikers, walkers, joggers, Rollerbladers, and dogs. We made many graphs charting all the data and analyzed them to find peak hours and other traffic patterns. We were also able to compare bike traffic on the path with bike traffic on the street and analyze the percentage of increased bicycle traffic as a result of building the path.

Making graphs is a worthwhile mathematical activity, but too often that is the extent to which math gets integrated into project-based learning. The exciting part, however, is when careful analysis of the data reveals something about the patterns of human activity. Appendix G is a sequence of charts and graphs prepared by one group of students as they moved from gathering raw data to interpreting the data.

Here's another example: We took our counts at five intersections

BOWMAN SCHOOL BIKE PATH QUESTIONNAIRE

1) Name _____

2) How do you use the bike path?

   ☐ Bike for recreation? ☐ Rollerblade? ☐ Jog? ☐ Walk?

   Other? _____

3) How often do you use the bike path?

   ☐ Everyday? ☐ Once a week? ☐ Once every two weeks? ☐ Once a month?

   Other? _____

4) Did you use the bike path before it was a bike path?

   ☐ Yes? ☐ No?

   For what? _____

5) How do you compare using the bike path to using the street?

   _____

6) Did you want this place to be a bike path?

   _____

7) Do you cut through abutters' yards?

   ☐ Yes? ☐ No?

8) How old are you? (Please circle.)

   1-10; 10-20; 20-30; 30-40; 40-50; 50-60; 60-70; 70-80.

9) Have you ever had any problems on the bike path?

   _____

10) Have you ever seen any wild animals? And what kind?

   _____

11) What's the most interesting thing you have seen on the bike path?

   _____

12) If you are an abutter, please write and tell us how you like living next to the bikepath.

   _____

The students in Mr. Levy's Fourth Grade Class thank you for taking the time to fill this out. Have a great day.

When done, please return this survey and your comments to:

Bowman School, 9 Phillip Road, Lexington 02173 (Attention: Room 9).

FIG. 9-2: *Bike path questionnaire*

where the bike path crossed a road. When we looked at the graphs we saw consistent traffic from one cross street to the other until suddenly the traffic diminished significantly. We hypothesized why this might be; then we looked at a street map of Lexington and realized that the center of town, where Steve's Ice Cream, the Coffee Connection, and many other stores are located, was in between one cross street, where fifty-six bikes crossed, and the next, where only thirteen were counted. We deduced that much of the traffic was stopping at these businesses. This hypothesis was corroborated by data collected by the group studying the effect of the path on local business, who found that sales were up twenty to thirty percent in the stores they contacted.

Or again: On a beautiful autumn day we counted 126 bikes during the peak hour. But on an equally beautiful day in the spring, we counted 276 bikes during the peak hour. What might account for the difference? Again, such data go beyond the making of graphs and challenge us to look for the meaning and understanding that the numbers can reveal. After much discussion and many hypotheses, we decided that in the fall people were tired of riding the bikes that they had been using all summer. In the spring, they couldn't wait to get out after being cooped up all winter.

Science and Service

One of my science requirements for fourth grade is simple machines. The bicycle provided the perfect opportunity to explore simple machines in action. I put a single-speed BMX bicycle in the back of the room and had one group take it apart. The next group put it back together. Then another group took it apart, and so on. They got pretty good at this, and one of the children suggested that we open up a bike shop: we could do simple tune-ups and repairs for children in the school. The children were excited by the idea, but it was January, so business was pretty slow. Someone then had the idea of fixing up old bikes. Maybe we could give them to children who didn't have bicycles. The children wrote a letter to the local newspaper explaining our project and asking for people to call us if they had a bike in

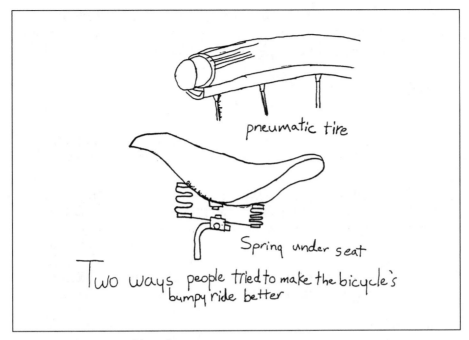

pneumatic tire

Spring under seat

Two ways people tried to make the bicycle's bumpy ride better

FIG. 9-3:   *Drawing of bicycle improvements*

their garage that no one used anymore. About twenty-five bikes were donated; the ones that were in really bad shape we used for parts.

We called a local bike shop and asked if they would send someone down to show us how they evaluate the condition of a bicycle. The owner of the store (Jerry Slack of the Cycle Loft in Burlington, Massachusetts) came to visit and was so impressed with what the children were doing that he gave us tools and bike repair equipment. He also showed us step by step how to check out a bicycle and determine what it needs. Steve Taranto, another local bike expert, allowed us to make a video of him as he evaluated the condition of a used bicycle. The video was a valuable resource when we were in the midst of repairing bicycles ourselves.

Every day the groups took turns working on the bicycles. While other groups were working on their research (see Figure 9–3), one group would be working on repairs. I was amazed that several girls and boys had never used a screwdriver before. Our biggest problem was locating the tools we needed, so one group took on the task of organizing a shelf with clear outlines and labels for all the tools.

Jeff hated school. I had visited him over the summer and he told me as much. His parents just accepted the fact. There wasn't much anybody could do about it.

The one time I saw Jeff get excited was when he showed me the trailer in his backyard that he and his dad had restored. I was amazed at what he knew about tools and what he could do with them. I took every opportunity to put his skills to work. When the teacher next door asked for help hanging chart paper, I sent Jeff over. When we needed a grow-lab for our plant study, I asked Jeff to build it for us. I organized a project for making pencil boxes so Jeff would feel school was a place for him. Every morning I asked him how he liked school. The most he ever gave me was "It's okay." His parents said that was a lot.

When the bike shop opened, Jeff found school was a place for him. He knew every tool, every part of the bike. He was the expert. Everyone went to Jeff whenever they needed help. He shined in the bike shop, but even more important, the confidence he gained helped him become a dedicated writer as he researched the effects of the bike path on the environment. I still never got any more than "Okay" from Jeff, but he said it with a smile and a twinkle in his eye. That was enough for me.

We never opened the store for tune-ups. It took us until the end of the year to repair the bicycles we had collected. We were able to restore eighteen bicycles but did not know who to give them to. I knew that if we couldn't find a connection, we could always give them to an orphanage, but I wanted the children to feel the joy of witnessing joy in others. I also wanted to avoid the syndrome of "rich kids" giving charity to the poor. My class had their own poverty, the poverty of gratitude.

Thinking about whom we might give the bikes to, I remembered my one-day teaching experience in Lawrence (see Chapter 7). I discussed the possibility of an exchange with Mrs. Retelle, a Lawrence teacher. My class was doing a project on wool, seeing how it got from the raw fleece to a finished piece of cloth. I knew that Lawrence used to be the wool capital of the world back at the turn of the century. I proposed to Mrs. Retelle that if her class would teach us about the history of Lawrence, my class would teach them about the American Revolution and the Battle of Lexington that began the war. She agreed.

The Lawrence class sent us wonderful stories and illustrations about the city of Lawrence. Our class did the same for them about Lexington. Pen pals were arranged and several letters went back and forth while we planned our visits. We would go to Lawrence for a tour of the mills. Then they would come to Lexington to see the Lexington Green and several historic buildings where significant events happened at the beginning of the American Revolution.

Our visit to Lawrence was outstanding. We met downtown at a historical park. We saw slides of Lawrence history, and the children had prepared an exhibit about all the special places in their town. They took us for a tour of the old mills and showed us the power of the mighty Merrimack, which turned the great water wheels that ran the looms.

Before the Lawrence class came to visit us in Lexington, Mr. Dooks, my student teacher, went to Lawrence and taught them about the Battle of Lexington. He gave them a script he had edited that portrayed the events of the battle as reconstructed by historians. Every year in April there is a reenactment of the battle on the Lexington Green. We decided to stage our own reenactment. Mr. Dooks taught the Lawrence students the maneuvers of the colonial militia; we taught our students the marching commands of the British "regulars."

We were very excited when it was time for the Lawrence students to visit us in Lexington. We planned to ride the bikes that we had restored to the Lexington Green, along the bike path of course, then give them to the Lawrence students at the end of the day. That morning we were all dressed in our British uniforms (mainly red shirts, white pants, and cardboard grenadier hats) and lined up on the playground with the eighteen bikes we had fixed. I, however, was having trouble participating in the excitement. There were twenty-one children in the Lawrence class, and we only had eighteen bikes. While my children were racing around on the bikes, testing them, I was rehearsing my speech. "Listen, we have saved the best bikes for you. They are not quite ready yet, but we will bring them to you when we are finished." I didn't know where we would get three more bikes, but I knew we would.

I had also been worried about helmets. Could we in good conscience give the bikes without helmets? It was a law in Massachusetts that children had to wear helmets. Two days before the Lawrence children were to visit us, I got a call from a woman who had heard about our bicycle repair project and had some old three-speed bikes up in a camp in New Hampshire. We could have them if we went up to get them. That didn't sound too promising, but as we talked further I found out she was the president of the Lexington Bicycle Safety Program and had in her attic boxes of old helmets left over from safety demonstrations. I told her about giving the bikes to the children of Lawrence, and she was delighted to give us the helmets to go along with them.

Just before we left to meet the Lawrence children, one of my students came up to me walking her bike. The gears didn't work. The derailleur was bent and needed major repairs. We didn't have time to work on it then, so my speech would now have to be delivered to four children.

We arrived on the Green and began to get into formation. Our drummer authoritatively accompanied the orders the captains repeatedly bellowed. "Quiet in the ranks!" was the one heard most frequently. Meanwhile, the Lawrence children were all in Buckman Tavern, where the original colonial Minutemen had gathered early in the morning of April 17, 1775. Finally, the colonial captain, a robust Latino, shouted, "The regulars are coming, the regulars are

Preparing for "battle" on the Lexington Green

coming!" and the Lawrence patriots, dressed in authentic colonial costumes they had procured from the Lawrence Historical Society, poured out of the tavern and assumed their positions on the Green. My class slowly advanced and we reenacted the battle that began the Revolutionary War. After the battle, we met the "enemy," and they were our pen pals.

I went to confess to Mrs. Retelle that we only had seventeen bikes. Before I could say anything, she said, "I don't know how many bikes you were able to fix, but only seventeen children brought permission slips to receive one." She was very surprised when I leapt into the air and shouted, "Hallelujah!"

We lined the bikes up according to size, and the Lawrence children did likewise. They stood behind their bikes, put on their helmets and prepared to ride around the Green. None of them had their own bike. One girl from Viet Nam had never been on a bicycle before.

My class could hardly imagine. The Lawrence children raced around the Green with unbounded delight, while my children watched with pride. We then enjoyed a great picnic together.

Sharing What We Learned

As the results of our research began to take form, we decided to produce a book to share what we had learned with the community. Some of the groups finished their section in a timely manner. Other groups had more difficulty getting information or writing about it. Finally I had to issue last call. All groups had to turn in whatever they had by the end of the week, and then we would assign a group of editors the task of finishing up and pulling all the different chapters together. Before I asked for volunteer editors, I warned them that they would have to come in before school, miss every recess, stay after school, take work home. I wanted to weed out all those who would not be willing to make the ultimate commitment. I got eighteen volunteers. I picked the most capable independent writers and titled them the writing editors. The second group were the copy editors. They read every word and checked for spelling, grammar, and punctuation. The rest became artistic editors. They were called on whenever a picture was needed. This seemed to satisfy everyone.

The book, *On the Path*, was not ready for printing until the last day of school, so we had to save our book-signing celebration until the next year. It was a grand signing indeed. We invited all the people who had helped us in our project—parents, town officials, townspeople. We had a few speeches from students, parents, and guests, and gave autographed copies of the book to all our honored visitors. Then each chapter committee sat behind a table to sell and sign books and to answer questions people had about their particular chapter.

Our project and the book we produced came to the attention of the Massachusetts Department of Environmental Management and the National Park Service, who recognized us as Conservation Heroes. The editors and I attended a dinner and ceremony in our honor. The National Park Service bought one hundred copies of *On the Path* to send to other communities across the country who were interested in converting existing railroad tracks into bike trails.

When I shared the project with a group of teachers, one of them acknowledged that it sounded interesting but asked how I could justify spending all year studying a bike path. What about the rest of the curriculum? Although the children learned much about the bike path, it was my intention to use their interest in something exciting and relevant to enliven the basic skills. We covered and went beyond much of the required fourth-grade curriculum. Content areas that did not correspond to the bike path study were covered separately. One student summed it up well two years after leaving my class. "We learned without really knowing we were learning," he said. "It was fun, and we don't usually associate learning with fun."

CHAPTER TEN

Discipline and Character

The success of projects like the ones described in this book depends on the kind of classroom we've created. One of the most potent opportunities we have to shape class culture is in managing social relationships; in handling disputes, conflicts, teasing, and the breaking of the rules, we demonstrate the values of freedom and justice.

The Art of Discipline

I never like to issue a consequence unless the child admits to the crime. If I punish someone without a confession, his heart will be hardened against me. If I didn't believe him, why should he listen to me? If I didn't trust his word, why should he trust mine? A child whose conscience lacks fine-tuning, even if she is lying, is hurt if I punish her for something she says she didn't do.

When the offender pleads not guilty and I have no way to prove otherwise, I talk to the parties involved. I assure the plaintiff that the offender didn't mean any harm and encourage her to tell me if anything like it occurs again. I tell the offender that he must have done something to bother her and to be more careful next time. I try to get them to talk to each other about it, and give them a protocol for doing so.

⁂

The thing about Charles is that he would never admit to having done anything wrong. Whenever anyone accused him of a misdemeanor, he would utterly and emphatically deny it.

Accusations against Charles happened regularly. I allowed my incredulity to grow more and more perceptible as the charges against Charles mounted. I could barely contain myself one day when he denied having spit on three girls.

The next day James came in from recess and said Charles had spit on his coat. He showed me the sleeve and there was a wet spot near the elbow with the unmistakable salivary froth still bubbling. I thought I had him.

"Charles, come here! James says you spit on his coat."

"I didn't do it."

"Charles, look at the wet spot on his sleeve. It still has the spit bubbles on it."

"Yeah, but that's not from me."

I took them into the hall. "Charles, why would James say you spit on him if you didn't?"

"I don't know."

"Could you have done it by accident, maybe? Sometimes spit comes out when we talk."

"No way."

"James, did anybody else see it?"

"Yeah, Jerry and Hector."

"Just a minute. I'll be right back." I left them in the hall to seek the witnesses.

"Jerry, did you see what happened between James and Charles?"

"Yeah, I saw Charles spit at James."

"Hector, did you see what happened between James and Charles?"

"Yeah, Charles spit at James."

"Thank you."

Back in the hall: "Charles, Jerry and Hector both say they saw you spit at James."

"But I didn't."

"Charles, these guys are your friends! It's not like the girls telling

147

on you for something to get you in trouble. Why would they say they saw you do it?"

"Maybe they want to get me in trouble."

I thought I had enough on Charles to make a case. If the evidence of the fresh spit mark and two witnesses was not enough to coax a confession, nothing ever would. I thought of threatening him with a DNA test to match his spit with the spit on the coat, but I was afraid he would call my bluff. I said, "Charles, it seems that one of two things is going on here, and I need to know which one before we go any further. Either it's your memory, I mean this all happened at least five minutes ago, maybe you did it and forgot. Or it could be that you are trying to deceive me because you are afraid of getting in trouble. Now I want you to stay out here and think about it and tell me when you decide. Because we will work on it differently, depending on whether it is a problem of memory or deception."

Charles puzzled over his choice. I suspect he couldn't figure out which answer would best get him off the hook. About fifteen minutes later I visited him in the hall.

"Well, Charles, have you made up your mind?"

"Yeah, I think it must be my memory." I guess that sounded better to him than deceit.

"Wonderful!" I said. "Now that's something we can work on."

The challenge in discipline is that you have to represent both grace and justice at the same time. The offender has usually acted out of a place of need. She needs to be inspired, uplifted, strengthened in confidence. If she is shamed in front of the class, the opposite effect is often achieved. On the other hand, the class needs to see that justice has been done, that a crime will not go unpunished. Often I use the secret chamber of the hall to administer the torture.

"Mr. Levy, John keeps shooting a rubber band at me."

I put on my stern face. "John, come here right now." We go out in the hall. The class snickers.

"Ha! He's getting it now."

Meanwhile, out in the hall: "John, whenever we are having a discussion and you raise your hand to speak, I can't wait to hear what you have to say. You bring such an interesting perspective to the class. This class needs your gifts. You are in this class for a special reason, and if you do not share your gifts with us, our class will never become what it is supposed to be and neither will you. Do you understand? Now c'mon, we need the best you have to give." John nods his assent. We walk solemnly back into the room. The class believes justice has been done, and John has been encouraged, built up. For many children with a tendency to be disruptive, that is all they need.

There are some, of course, who need more. When I do proclaim a punishment for an offense, there are three things I try to keep in mind. First, the punishment must fit the crime. Detention, extra math homework, or going to the principal's office are not usually the most natural consequences of an infraction. Children have a fierce sense of justice, and their healthy intuitions about what is fair will not be nourished if they cannot sense the relationship between the punishment and the crime. If they do discern the connection, they will be more likely to endure the sentence with relative cooperation and, on occasion, even satisfaction.

If a child is not listening in class, I might give him an assignment to spend some time that night in a quiet place and practice listening: "Write down everything you hear in twenty minutes." (That assignment produced Figure 10–1.) If a child goofs off during a song, I may have her write the words to the song in calligraphy and frame it on the wall. If one child harms another, I have him do something kind or make something beautiful for the child he hurt.

The second thing I try to keep in mind when I discipline a child is that I want to give her a chance for full redemption, in her own eyes and in the eyes of her peers. I want her to have an opportunity to balance whatever destructive deed was done with an act of goodness. If a child reenters the community without having had a chance to be redeemed, he returns weaker than when he left. His self-esteem lowered, shamed in the eyes of his classmates, he will likely act out again, if only to prove he is above all this school stuff anyway; he

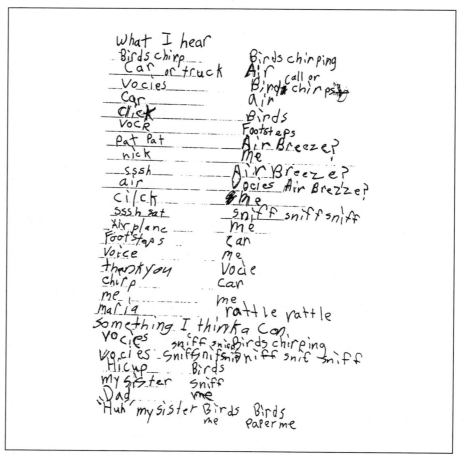

FIG. 10-1:   *A student practices listening*

doesn't care. So we must make sure that the child is able to come back strong, fully forgiven. An important response to any apology by an offender is forgiveness by the victim. One without the other does not resolve the conflict.

Finally, I try to administer discipline, in the fourth grade anyway, with a light touch. A bit of humor goes a long way. For example, I have a bell I ring to signal silence. If a child continues talking I might ask her to provide a meal for the bell, which is obviously weak—since she didn't hear it—and in need of nourishment. The bell feeds on the adoring compliments of its subjects. Some of the most wonderful writing my children have produced has been letters or poems to the bell (see Figure 10–2). Of course I read them with great ceremony, and place the bell on the written paper for complete digestion.

Here are some other examples:

1. A child who calls another "snotface" writes a report on mucus and delivers it to the class.
2. A child who has a bad habit of shouting a certain four-letter word writes an ode to manure.
3. A girl caught chewing gum for the ten-zillionth time writes a letter to Mr. Wrigley, blaming him for making the gum so tasty that she can't resist.

These extra assignments are done during the child's free time (at recess or as extra homework), so while we have fun with them, something productive is created by the offender and justice is represented to the rest of the class.

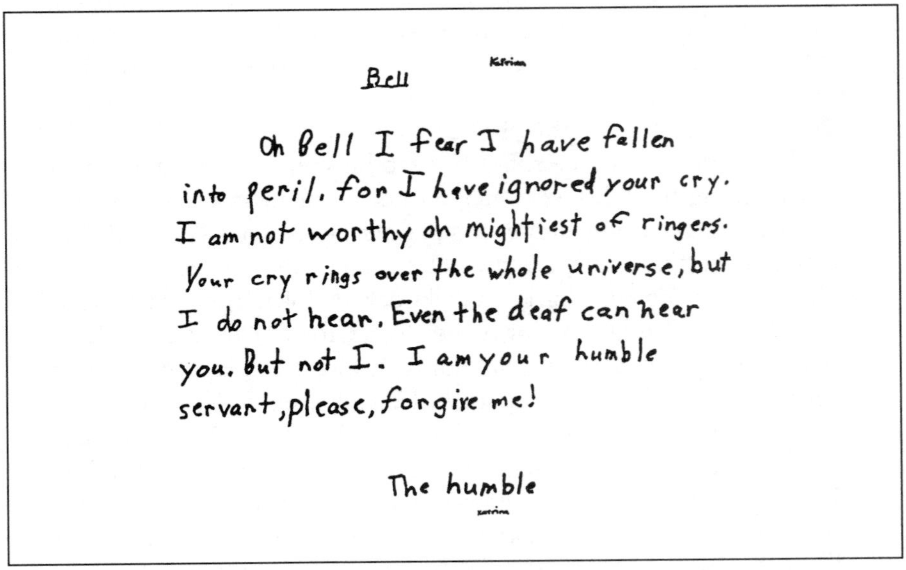
Bell

Oh Bell I fear I have fallen
into peril. for I have ignored your cry.
I am not worthy oh mightiest of ringers.
Your cry rings over the whole universe, but
I do not hear. Even the deaf can hear
you. But not I. I am your humble
servant, please, forgive me!

The humble

FIG. 10-2: *A "meal" for the bell*

When I cannot think of a meaningful consequence in the heat of the battle, I tell the child I will talk to him later, which gives me some time to think of an appropriate response. You can't talk to some children directly after an altercation anyway, they are still too "hot." Sometimes I even wait until the next day. We are both likely to be able to look at the situation with more objectivity after a night's sleep.

———————————— ❧ ————————————

I did not have a problem thinking up something for Charles. I had been waiting too long. I found a long, beautiful sonnet by Shakespeare. "Charles, we begin our memory work today. When we are done, you will have the best memory in the class. I want you to begin by memorizing this poem."

"The whole thing?!"

"The whole thing, of course. You may use your free time at recesses and at home. When you have mastered it, I think your memory will be good enough for me to let you out during recess again."

It took a week and a half. He almost made it a few times, missing a line or a few words, but I insisted it be perfect. When he was done, he recited it before the class. His embarrassment turned to pride as he sensed the reaction of the class. Everyone was amazed. Charles had stature in the class he never had before.

I let him out for recess, but insisted he keep a log for a few days of everything he did. Just to make sure the memory was working.

I didn't have any more complaints about Charles until late winter. Four girls from another class came into my room before school and claimed Charles had knocked down their snow fort. "Charles, did you knock down their snow fort?" I tried everything to prevent Charles from responding before he had a chance to carefully think about the question. I could see the denial ready to burst from his lips. I made him go until 3:00 p.m. without responding, reminding him throughout the day of the importance of telling the truth, assuring him I would not punish him unjustly. As I shook his hand at the end of the day I asked him, "Charles, did you knock down the snow fort?" I think he had stored up too much stock in his feigned innocence.

"No, I didn't touch their fort."

I was crushed. "Okay, Charles, we'll talk about it tomorrow."

I didn't sleep well that night, and when morning came I still didn't have a plan. When I saw Charles that morning I took him aside. "Have you changed your mind?" I asked him hopefully. "Did you remember anything in your sleep?"

His eyes looked down at the ground. "No, I didn't do it."

"Okay, Charles, I'll talk to you later."

I went and sought out the four girls who had reported the incident. I interviewed them separately, and each one told the exact same story. They knew what he was wearing, the order of his actions, and even the words he spoke when they begged him to leave it alone.

When recess time came, I called Charles aside. "Last chance, did you do it?"

"No, I told you." What he meant was, I don't think there is any way any adult saw me and could prove it.

"Well, Charles, let me tell you something about the way justice works in America." I went on to explain our court system and how the different sides get to tell their story before the jury and then the jury decides. "Now Charles, if it was just your word against one other person it would be difficult to decide who was telling the truth. But in this case, there are four girls and they each told me the exact same story about what you did! There is no way a jury would take your word over four different people. So I am going to nail you."

"But what if I didn't do it?"

"Well, I figure even if you didn't do it, there are so many things you did do that you never got caught for that this will just barely begin to even the record."

The reason for the fort, it turns out, was because the third-grade class was making books for our sister city in Nicaragua. The children there had no books, nor did they have snow. So the class was going to take pictures of the snow fort and send them in a book to the Nicaraguan children. They had already written the text, but there was one problem: the children of Nicaragua speak Spanish, and the books were in English.

After Charles rebuilt the fort for the class (which was too much fun) I had him translate the book into Spanish. Fourth graders in our school take Spanish, so I thought this would be an excellent opportunity to practice using what he had learned. He had to try it all himself, and then he was allowed to ask for help from the Spanish teacher.

When the translation was complete, I had him write every page in calligraphy. He presented it to the third grade after having spent two weeks of recess working on it. They were almost as pleased as Charles was.

Building Individual Character

The debate about character education continues in our schools and communities. Some say that it is essential for schools to return to teaching basic values, that our straying away from educating character is a major factor in producing today's terrible social ills. Others claim that our schools must be value neutral because of the tremendous diversity of our students and the vastly divergent values they bring into the classroom. Besides, who is qualified to decide which values should be taught? Therefore we should keep our hands off values altogether and stick to the business of learning.

I think both sides miss the essential point, namely, that we *are* teaching values, and cannot escape teaching values, all day, every day. We cannot avoid it even if we want to! Every decision we make, every judgment we administer, every interaction with a child, demonstrates what we value and serves as a model for our students about what really counts in life, in being human. Every curriculum choice, every pedagogical method, every assessment, reveals what we consider important. All our decisions serve as influential models to children, whose dispositions, habits, and perspectives are formed under our care.

For example, take the issue of how we conduct our lessons. Do we lecture to the students and expect them to memorize what we say? If so, what does that indicate about our view of children, of learning, of what is important? What different implications are communicated to our students when we teach through inquiry? Our values are implicitly expressed in how we run our classrooms. They show in what subjects we teach, how we teach them, and in what we exhibit on the walls of the room. The children take all this in day after day, as unconsciously as breathing. It all works in subtle ways in the formation of their character.

The word *character* comes from its Latin equivalent meaning *mark, sign, distinctive quality*. Its Middle English derivation meant *to cut into furrows; to engrave*. The modern definition that most closely matches its original use is *main or essential nature; strongly marked and serving to distinguish*. Does that sound familiar? Isn't this definition of character close to the definition of genius—essential spirit, that quality that makes something what it is—that we began with in Chapter 1? When we help children develop their genius, we are helping them build character.

Our character is the sum of our habits. It has to do with our most basic modes of perception and expression. It is not learned like facts in geography or science. Habits that form character are only established through repeated and continuous practice. They are not things one thinks are good ideas and adopts. They become part of the very fabric of one's being; they become automatic dispositions and responses.

Stan had a disposition that automatically avoided work. Whenever confronted with an assignment he did not feel like doing, he went into a long series of moves to avoid it. Deep inside him was an escape artist. All his energy and creativity went into getting out of the work, and he had enjoyed great success over the years. One day I asked him to copy over a draft of a paragraph he was writing onto "book" paper. First, he refused as a simple matter of fact. This was his first move. "I don't want to."

"That's all right, you don't have to *want* to, you just have to do it."

His next move was defiant. "I'm not gonna do it, and you can't make me!"

"Well," I said calmly, "if you don't get to it before recess, you can use your recess to finish it."

Then he went into his cool act, saving face in front of the other children. He shrugged his shoulders and laughed. "Who cares? It's too cold to go out to recess anyway."

After recess we moved on to another subject, and I suppose Stan thought he had escaped. When lunchtime came, I asked him if he had finished copying over his paper. He hadn't, of course, so I invited him to use his lunch recess to complete the task. He sensed at this point that this might be a serious battle. He moved to the next level of defense, which was a stream of very genuine, very moving tears. It was clear how he had managed to get his way in the past: one move or another would eventually defeat his adversary. But I also saw how important it was for someone to care enough to go the distance, to establish the authority he longed for and free him from the tyranny of his own feelings.

"I am sorry you feel that way," I consoled him. "But I am sure it won't take you longer than ten minutes to finish. If you get started right away you will still have time for plenty of recess." He continued sobbing, his head down on his desk and buried under his coat.

At the end of the day Stan had still not finished his work. How far could I go? I thought one last threat would inspire him to do the job. "Shall I call your mom and tell her you won't be coming home on the bus today?" I asked. His next move was a kind of emotional suicide. He went limp and mumbled something like, "I don't care what you do to me," sank down into his chair, and refused to react to anything I said.

"Okay," I said. "I'll call your mom and tell her you need a little more time to finish your work." I called Stan's mother and explained what was happening. Fortunately, she supported me; I told her I would bring him home when he finished the work.

When the final bell sounded, there was Stan, crumpled on his desk with no intention of doing anything. After the other children had gone, I tried to break through the barrier, but he still would not let me in. I thought maybe if I left him alone he would take care of business. "Stan, I have a meeting with some other teachers. I'll be next door. Come and see me when you have finished, and I'll give you a ride home." I did not really have a meeting, but I arranged one on the spot with my neighbor in the next room. I left the door open so I could peek in and monitor Stan's progress. But, alas! There wasn't any.

Finally, at five o'clock I was ready to go home. "C'mon Stan, this is your last chance," I said, with, for the first time, a bit of bite in my voice. "I need to get home. Let's finish this now and get out of here." No response. This was the bottom line. I went down to the kindergarten and got a cot that they used for nap time. I set it up in the room. "Listen, Stan," my voice calm again, "I have to go home now. Make sure that you turn off the lights and turn down the heat before you go to bed. I think you will be all right here. I'll tell your mom you decided to sleep over at school. I'll be back early in the morning and we'll see how you did." I put my coat on and went down to the office to check my mail. On my way back down the hall, there was Stan in the middle of the hall.

"I'm done, Mr. Levy, I'm done." It wasn't a great job. It had taken him all of three minutes to copy the paragraph over. I decided not to make him correct the spelling error I spotted in the third line. We would get to that tomorrow.

"Great job, Stan. Let's go home."

Sometimes an old habit has to be broken before a new one can be formed. I knew that until Stan was able to overcome his propensity to avoid work, he would remain a slave to his emotions; he would be unable to call forth the will needed to master his feelings at any given moment. He would work when he felt like it, avoid it when he didn't.

Good character is often won in overcoming how we happen to feel in any given moment. It is developed by going against the grain. Children feel a sense of strength and power when they are able to accomplish something they did not feel they could do. I needed to help Stan realize that even though he did not feel like copying over his paper, he could do it for the simple reason that it was his responsibility at the time. I had to establish the unyielding expectation that he would succeed.

Stan never went through the litany of his escape tactics with me again. He seemed as if a great weight had been lifted from his shoulders. I don't think anyone had ever gone the distance with him before. I never had to again.

CHAPTER ELEVEN

Exit Signs

When teachers read about other teachers' incredible work, like the book I just finished on David Millstone's *Odyssey* project, it is easy to feel overwhelmed. How can the children do all that outstanding work? How does the teacher know so much about the subject matter? How could he organize such a vast variety of activities? Even if we have the courage to try to replicate such an activity, frustration surfaces when we find it does not work in our classrooms.

"It must be because he is in a small school."

"Those are fifth graders, mine are only fourth."

"He must get a lot more support from his parents and administrators."

"It may work in Vermont, but not here in the city."

"My kids just aren't capable of doing it."

"He must have forgotten to tell me something when he described the project."

I don't want anyone who might try to incorporate any of the ideas in this book to be disappointed or discouraged, so I want to make sure no one gets stuck looking at my finger instead of where it is pointing. I discovered another problem with pointing one afternoon while I was trying to find an alternative route to the airport to avoid horrendous traffic on the expressway. Signs with airplanes at strategic intersections pointed which way to turn, guiding me through the unfamiliar maze of Revere and Chelsea. And then the signs stopped.

I went for a long way down littered streets and past boarded-up buildings, anxiously awaiting the next sign, but I never found it. Perhaps it was a cruel trick. Maybe some kids took a sign down to confuse drivers. Maybe I just missed it. Whatever it was, I was lost. And I probably would have made it to the airport faster if I had gone the familiar way, even with all the traffic. Therefore, as a teacher giving directions how to get from one way of teaching to another, I want to make sure I don't leave out anything crucial.

I want to erect three signs for anyone who may be inspired to try to implement any of the ideas from this book in his or her classroom. The first has to do with building the kind of community from which these kinds of projects are most likely to emanate. The second is a word about beginning small. The third is about the need for teachers to be examples of what we want to teach to the children. These are your "exit signs" as you leave this book and chart your own road.

Building Community

The kind of learning I describe in this book is built on a powerful sense of classroom community. This is a big sign; you can't miss it. I don't believe any of the projects I have outlined would have been possible if each person in the room hadn't felt she or he was part of a supportive community, where respect and care kindled confidence in one another's strengths and empathy for one another's weaknesses.

It is risky to teach in a way that is open to a new idea or direction that may come at any moment from a question or comment someone offers in class. There are no prepared lessons, no activities, and sometimes, no knowledge about where one is going. The only reason I am able to take that risk is because of the quality of the community we have built. I know that the spirit, the genius of the class, will find a way through any obstacle. And not just *any* way, but a way full of excitement, discovery, and challenge. I also have faith that I will be able to connect my students' excitement to the core of the required curriculum. I have learned that when you dig deep enough or wide enough you find meaningful connections between all things.

How, then, do we build a sense of community in the class? The best way is to be weird. At least this is what the children call it, and they usually intend it as a compliment. It means that a teacher is different from what they are used to. Teachers can earn the designation *weird* or its cousins, *alien* and *psycho*, by allowing their enthusiasms and eccentricities full rein.

I once had a reunion with a class two years after they had graduated from fourth grade. I wanted to hear what they remembered. I wondered if anything they learned in fourth grade had carried on beyond that year. Here's what I found out:

- They were able to articulate my interdisciplinary approach: "We liked the way you mooshed all the subjects together."
- They caught the authentic nature of the curriculum: "We got to apply the stuff you taught us to real life. I mean, like, it wasn't just in a, like, book."
- They appreciated the way we involved the community: "We worked harder and more carefully because we thought that people out there cared about what we did."

I was gratified that they could express these things, but not entirely surprised. Those had, after all, been my intentions. However, I was totally surprised by a comment one child made: "We could really be ourselves in your class."

I pressed her on the point, to find out what subtle factors I might have employed to create this nurturing environment in which they could be themselves. "What was it about the class that allowed you to feel you could be yourself? Why didn't you feel you could be yourself in other classes?"

"Well, we usually feel pretty weird," she said, "so when we saw how weird you were, it made us feel right at home, like we could be ourselves."

"Yeah," echoed another, "it was like there was no standard of sanity."

So much for my ingenious teaching techniques. But it does illustrate the importance of creating a unique environment to liberate the uniqueness of each of its inhabitants.

Teachers have a paradoxical challenge. We certainly want to develop the individuality in each child. But we also need to help each one learn to function as a member of a larger community. Can we lead the children to find their own individuality within the context of a group? Can we educate them to understand that their true individuality is what unites them rather than separates them from one another? Can we guide them to recognize that their personal gifts and strengths are for the good of the community and not just to advance their own cause? These are the "grand" questions at the heart of my teaching. Building a community of strong individuals is my greatest challenge. All the learning projects depend on it.

A child's first education in community life is the family. For some children there will be much guidance and good role modeling in learning the joys and struggles of community life: learning how to share, how to take turns, how to offer help, how to ask for help, how to be responsible, how to set aside personal desires for the good of the group. Other children will have to find a sense of community with little, or even negative, guidance and role modeling from family members. This intensifies the challenge of building community in the classroom.

Whatever sense of community our children bring to school, the classroom is their next important experience and training in community life. It is the next practice ground for living together in the world. The teacher has a major impact in awakening the sense of community in each child. The attention we pay to functioning as a classroom community is essential in preparing our students to enter the larger communities of our town, our nation, and our world. What can the teacher do to build community in the classroom?

Honor for the Individual

If a child does not feel honored as an individual, he or she will not be able to function as a responsible member of the group. By honor, I really mean recognizing a child's genius as described earlier. I expect the best from each child in every endeavor. I find something to praise in whatever the child is able to produce and challenge her to stretch to the next level. Finally, I assist her with whatever resources are necessary to get her there. A child who feels honored as an individual will be more likely to be a healthy presence in the community.

I have developed a variety of other ways to honor each child. I visit every family in their home before the school year begins. I find out each child's special interests and draw on them throughout the year to keep him or her involved or make the curriculum relevant. I also try to determine the parents' values, their hopes and concerns for their child. I am an assistant to the parents. The responsibility to educate the child is theirs; I am there to help them in that formidable task. I cannot truly educate the child without involving the family. Sometimes, one step with the parents is worth ten with the child. The children will feel more secure in school when they know their parents and teachers are working together. It is very difficult to command the respect of the child if the teacher does not have it from the parents.

At the beginning of every school day I shake the children's hands and greet each one as he or she enters the room. "Good morning, Marcus. I am looking forward to the thoughts that will come out of your mind today. I noticed that yesterday you brought much attention to yourself. But alas, it was for doing silly things. You fell off your chair, you made funny faces. I would like to see you call attention to yourself today by the power of your thinking. I will be listening to hear a thought from you that will make us all notice Marcus and go 'Wow!'"

I shake their hands again at the end of the day and reflect for a moment on any significant events that happened. "Alan, I was very impressed by how you gracefully admitted to throwing the paper airplane in class and didn't try to blame it on someone else. This is the beginning of dignity."

"Rosa, I was very impressed in math today when you didn't understand the problem and you asked a question. I would rather have a good question from you than the right answer. Keep up the good work."

In all our discussions I recognize whatever thoughts the children bring and start our journey to clarity and understanding from there. I protect incorrect or unformed thoughts from ridicule by classmates.

My students have to know I care about everything they do and that I will encourage and protect them as I draw out the best they have to give. When children feel their thoughts are respected, they're willing to take risks before the group. The community becomes a safe place for learning.

Ritual and Ceremony

Individual will is strengthened by repetition. Character is built in establishing habits. For example, if I make my bed every morning, I develop my will. No matter how I feel, how many excuses I can think of not to, I make my bed. I learn to act on the basis of something other than my feelings and desires of the moment. The character of the community is also strengthened by repetition. Ceremonies and rituals are the habits of community life. I begin every day with a song, and the community draws strength from the sacrifices each individual makes to join in no matter how they feel about singing on that particular morning. I set high expectations, and make sure all my students sing. If even one child does not join in, the community is weakened. We sing and recite poetry for twenty to thirty minutes to start each day. On the first day, I just start singing. The children listen until they begin to catch the words and then they join in—tentatively, reluctantly at first. They are generally too embarrassed to sing in front of each other. "Mr. Levy, this is what we did in kindergarten!" they moan. Singing, then, often becomes my first battleground for the minds and hearts of my students. Will they overcome their individual inhibitions in the spirit of the community effort? Will the defiant ones refuse to participate? Will the clowns sabotage the songs with humorous antics? Will the self-conscious or shy ones hold back in fear? The entire course of the year depends on this battle. For a week or two, I'm not always sure who is winning. I sing loud, maybe a few children join me, and the rest are still barely audible. But as they get to know the words, as they see I am not going to give up, as I give the resisters and detractors extra time to practice during recess, they gradually let themselves go. They become "young" again. The third week the music begins to sound beautiful. We get into harmony and rounds. I love rounds because the children have to concentrate on their part while listening to others sing theirs. This intense attention and concentration builds a focusing power that serves them well when they get to math class.

At the same time I introduce them to singing, I lead them in poetry recitation. At first we practice alliteration. I use short poems that emphasize each consonant. They are fun and especially energetic. I encourage the children to totally exaggerate each sound. "The *tutor* who *tooted* the *flute* . . ." "*Blossoms beautiful* and *bright* . . ." I tell them if they explode the *B* properly it should knock me back a step. I insist on hearing the *d* at the end of *and*, and the *t* in the middle of *beautiful*. We have a verse for every consonant in the alphabet. Their speech is generally sloppy, which I suspect causes some problems in spelling. "Just sound it out," we tell them. But they don't pronounce the words correctly, so sounding it out can be misleading.

Then we begin to learn some longer poems, rich in rhythm and alliteration, which makes them easier to memorize. I do not show the students the words. They have to learn them by listening to me and repeating. I know learning by rote is frowned on in most circles of education reform, but I find it valuable for two reasons.

First, their memory is exercised. The capability to memorize is powerful during the elementary years, but generally neglected. I am amazed how much and how fast children can memorize. They have the poems mastered long before I can put down my notes and join them. I hear reports from parents about how their children recite poems and songs at family events or in the car, all the way to New Hampshire!

Second, teaching poetry this way enables certain students who do not learn well visually, who may have difficulty reading, to excel. These students, keen listeners who remember everything they hear, have this rare opportunity to shine as leaders in the class. Whenever we get to a new stanza, Joseph or Sarah, both identified as needing extra help in reading, is right there to lead the way. The rest of the class waits for their lead. I have known many children over the years who found their genius in the memorization and dramatic recitation of poetry.

I also introduce playing the recorder during this morning time. I don't know how to read recorder music, so once again, they learn by watching me. We begin with simple, familiar melodies and soon advance to playing complicated rounds and harmonies. Playing the recorder is good for finger dexterity, small muscle control, and breathing and offers the joy of being able to produce beautiful sounds. This activity, like the poetry and singing, is perceived as Mr. Levy's "weirdness" and serves to distinguish our class as a unique community.

Finally, I use this beginning morning time to practice rhythmic exercises in balance, poise, coordination, and concentration. These exercises involve marching, clapping, balancing, or juggling, all done in chorus. That is important, because throughout all these morning activities, the point is for the individual *not* to be noticed. I don't want to hear any one voice when we sing, I want to hear a perfect blending. I don't want to see anyone stand out in the movement exercises, I want to see everyone moving in perfect harmony with the group. I suspect we have something to learn from the army in this regard. All these group activities provide opportunities for the children to practice finding their own individualities in the midst of the community. There will be plenty of other occasions for them to express their unique personality in the course of the day.

This time is also valuable for setting high standards. I insist that every note, every sound, counts and that we will not stop until we have performed together to the best of our ability. The students begin to pay attention to details they never noticed before. These same high standards we set for working together carry over into our academic pursuits and everything else we do in class.

The final way these morning rituals help build community is by breaking down the personas that many of the children have crafted to hide behind. They are all compelled to overcome inhibition, insecurities, and to act like "little children." They are loosened from the tougher, cooler images they all try hard so hard to project. There is already enough in the world that forces our children to grow up too fast. I encourage my students to be children, in the best sense of the word: the childlikeness so many adults would love to be able to reclaim in their own relationship with the world. I do everything I can to slow down the process of growing up, turning cynical, and especially getting cool.

I also try to protect my classroom from popular culture. Part of establishing a unique community is separating ourselves from the trends and fads of daily life. I do not sing many songs the children are familiar with. Most of my songs are from the folk tradition, from different cultures, or famous classics ("Ode to Joy," not "Louie, Louie"). We sing a lot of songs in Latin and other languages. My students rarely discuss what they saw on television or at the movies, not because I don't allow it, but rather because it is clear that our class belongs to a different world. I love Neil Postman's idea of education as a thermostat. When the temperature gets cold outside, the thermostat clicks on the heat. When the temperature outside gets hot, the thermostat clicks on the cold. That is the role, he claims, education should play in our society. It should offer an alternative, even an antidote, to the popular tendencies and fads of the time.

The best example I know of the thermostat principle was implemented by John F. Gardner, headmaster of a private school on Long Island. During the 1950s, when Joe McCarthy was accusing many people of being Communists and a spirit of intense nationalism energized American patriotism, Gardner did not require his students to say the pledge of allegiance every morning. But in the late 1960s and early 1970s, when there was great disrespect for the flag and a significant anti-American sentiment throughout the land, he had them say the pledge every morning.

You may have an entirely different approach to building community in your classroom. I respect that. What counts for learning in the way I have described is that the class feels they are a unique community, that they can accomplish great things when they work together. I encourage you to fill your classrooms with things you love, ideas you are interested in, activities you love to do. This will give a definite character to your classroom. It will make it distinct. It will make your students feel they are part of something special.

Celebrations

Celebrating together always helps develop a sense of community. Sharing the fruit of our labors is one way of celebrating our accomplishments. After singing and reciting poetry for several months, by Thanksgiving we have mastered a substantial amount of material. We take pride in showing the community what we have learned. We share our songs and poems at a school assembly and again when we invite all our parents and friends to a celebration on the last day before the vacation. I say *share* instead of *perform*, because it is really just doing for our friends and parents what we do every day in class. We have these celebrations throughout the year, usually on the last day before each vacation, when we have mastered a new set of poems and songs.

We also have dramatic performances each year. The stage offers a great outlet for our exercises in speech and movement. A dramatic production, although harrowing to organize, is a significant opportunity to set individual expression in the context of community achievement. I like to do at least one major production each year. We have written an opera based on our ideas of the creation and a play telling the story of the Mahabarata. We also perform an annual battle between King Winter and Queen Spring.

Celebrating Spring with the Maypole Dance

The practice of sharing what we do with the community is a big part of celebrating our classroom culture. We are strengthened by producing great products. If we sing in a concert for our parents, our bond is strengthened. If we produce a play and perform it for the rest of the school, our unity is intensified. If we design an exhibit that we show in a local museum, our pride as a class is enhanced. If we publish a book about something we explored together, we are knit together by the accomplishment. Producing great work that takes the collaboration of everyone is essential in building a strong sense of community.

There are many other opportunities for celebration throughout the day. I celebrate when a child makes a particularly enlightened comment, asks a deep and insightful question, or notices a significant correspondence between something we did in science and something in music or between something in math and a personal experience. We have a mood in the class of celebration when we make interesting connections between things or ideas.

We also celebrate important discoveries. We celebrate the gear when we see how it turns the energy from vertical to horizontal at the mill. We celebrate the chain on the bicycle when we understand how it made the high-wheeler obsolete. It is not that we do particular activities to celebrate these discoveries; rather the *mood* of our learning can be characterized by celebration. Every time we solve a problem that at first seemed to have no solution we have a feeling of joy and achievement.

We celebrate seasonal milestones: the first snow, the last leaf on the oak tree. These great simple events take precedence over our daily routine, and we take time to honor them with writing or song.

One unique celebration in my classroom occurs every time two children have the same thought. I am always disturbed when in the midst of a discussion I see one child drop her hand and mumble in disappointment, "Awww, that's what I was going to say!" The first time that happens each year, I stop everything.

"Excuse me," I say with incredulity, "what did you say? Did I see you drop your hand and mumble something?"

"Paul said my idea. That's what I was going to say."

"And that makes you groan and mumble? Excuse me; can you tell me how many thoughts might be going on in your mind at any given time? Can you count them?"

"Uh, no," she responds, entirely puzzled.

"And how many thoughts might Paul have in his mind?"

"I don't know," she says.

"Do you mean to tell me that of all the thoughts in the world, the same thought went into your mind and into Paul's mind at the same time? That is incredible! And you respond by mumbling and groaning? This is a time for rejoicing. It's amazing! From now on, whenever that happens, whenever someone else has the same thought as you, you must stand up and say, 'Rejoice!'" Throughout the rest of the year, many of our discussions are punctuated by the rejoicing of like-minded classmates.

Sometimes, after important accomplishments, like the finishing of our desks, we give a whole day over to celebration. We prepare poems, songs, dances, rituals, contests, and treats. Sometimes the

Rejoice!

public is invited, sometimes it's just us. But one thing is sure: celebration builds community, and we don't do enough of it in our classrooms.

Recognition of Others

At the root of community life is the recognition of the Other. To experience the fullness of community life, children need to develop empathy for other people—to rejoice in their joys and weep with their sorrows. Teachers need to awaken children's awareness of all the people who are at work on their behalf to make the school, town, nation, world a better place to live. We write letters to the secretary and custodian at the beginning of the year, thanking them for spending the summer preparing for our return. We write thank-you letters to everyone we can think of. Thank you, mailman. Thank you, garbage collector. Thank you, cafeteria helpers. We say a verse every morning: "We thank all those seen and unseen who make it possible for us to be here. . . ." We receive much from the larger community, and we also look for ways we can contribute to the school, town, state, country, world, all the communities we inhabit.

Beginning Small

The second exit sign I want to leave you with is a reminder, especially to beginning teachers, that projects like these take time to develop. I have been working on these ideas for over twenty years. No one should be overwhelmed by the magnitude of some of the projects I have described or frustrated if they have to implement a project on a smaller scale when trying it for the first time. Many of the projects I have done with my classes have developed over time. When I first began teaching, I worked in a private school that didn't use textbooks, so I was forced to develop my own curriculum from the very beginning. And because I stayed with the same class as the school expanded, I had to plan new curriculum every year.

When I taught in the public school, I worked my way through the required curriculum in as creative a way as possible. The wheat project was my first experience in seizing a teachable moment and developing it into a project. The first year it took most of my energies just to get the wheat into the ground. The mathematical, scientific, and historical integration was primitive. I was more concerned with figuring out how to organize it so no one got bashed with a shovel. The project developed further in successive years. As I got more familiar with the process, collected a variety of resources, and established an organizational framework, I was able to spend more time planning ways to tie it into the curriculum and to use the experience of growing wheat to develop skills and understanding in the different disciplines. Each year a new component was added, and the project fit into the curriculum in a different way. For example, one year the bread became the central project, involving activities in math, science, art, reading, and writing. Another year, we just planted the seed, processed the berries, and baked the bread without trying to connect it to other curriculum subjects. Another year the bread became a dividend for the investors who had bought shares to fund the building of our classroom furniture.

The wool project is another example of how curriculum is built up and fit together in different ways over the years. One year it was the central focus of our work for a season, and I expected everyone to participate in every step of the process. Another year I introduced working with wool as an extra opportunity for anyone who was interested. As you create projects over time, you develop a rich assortment of activities that can fit together to produce new and exciting patterns of curriculum. You increase the opportunities to find activities that will draw out the genius in each child. It is important to see your curriculum as developing over time. The hard work it takes the first time you attempt any project is like investing money in the bank. In successive years you will have rich resources to draw on when you need them.

Start with something small, something you love, something the children express an interest in, and expand and refine it from year to year.

Teacher as Example

The last exit sign relates to something I have referred to several times throughout the book. It is so obvious that I feel obligated to point it out, because we have a tendency to assume the obvious and ignore it. Before we can effectively draw anything out of our students, we have to draw it out of ourselves. I am embarrassed sometimes at the hypocrisy of trying to teach our students the values and skills that we have not developed in our own lives, either individually or collectively in our school communities. We are supposed to teach our children cooperative learning, but are we able to cooperate in our own faculty meetings? We are supposed to teach toleration of differences. How tolerant are we of colleagues down the hall who teach their classes in ways totally different from our own? We are supposed to teach creative problem solving. Do teachers ever have opportunities to solve problems in our school together?

If we try to teach our students something we have not experienced and developed in ourselves, they will not take us seriously. Children can always tell the difference between an idea we bring to class from a workshop we have attended or a book we have read and one that grows from our own striving and experience. Our authority comes from having applied an idea or principle in our own lives. This authority is what causes the children to listen to our words and trust what we say. Two teachers can say the exact same words, and one might have a great effect on the children while the other is ignored. The importance of teaching from our own experience and striving cannot be emphasized enough. Our "authentic" authority in the classroom comes not from being bigger or having the title of teacher but from having worked in ourselves to develop the qualities and skills we want to teach our children. As teachers, we need to be examples of the qualities we want to inspire in our students. All the fantastic curriculum, methods, and ideas for reform that have ever been created do not add up to this old adage: we teach more by who we are than by what we say.

We need to be examples not only in our character but also in our development of curriculum. What does it take to be able to escape from textbooks and develop the kind of curriculum described in this book?

When I think about teaching a particular subject, like writing, the first thing that comes to mind is that I have to be a practitioner of writing myself. In order to teach writing effectively, I have to be a writer. Only in writing myself do I gain insight into the subtleties of the writing process. I know how a few unrelated observations recorded in a journal can come together to make a wonderful story. I experience what it is like to have absolutely nothing to say or to capture an event with words and images so exquisite that the reader has an experience as powerful as being there. I know the laborious struggle of editing over and over again until the piece has a voice of its own and says what I really want it to say. Most important, when I speak to my students about writing out of my own experience, my words have authority.

If teachers need to practice writing to teach writing, what do we have to practice to develop good curriculum? What qualities do we need to nurture in our own lives to prepare us for developing curriculum in our classes?

Learning begins with observations. The first thing we need to do is to develop an eye for observation. We need to take notice of the things in the world around us. We see leaves turn colors, days get longer, the moon get fuller. Like Copernicus, we see the sun appear to move through the sky. Like Isaac Newton, we see an apple fall from a tree. We see people shopping, jogging, crying, celebrating. We see advertisements, buses, and bridges. We read about all manner of events in newspapers and magazines. But in the midst of such rich fields of observation, we often walk through our days checking off our lists, taking care of business, without taking time to reflect, digest, or wonder about any of the mysteries that surround us. To prepare ourselves to help our children learn from their own observations, we first have to take hold of what we observe around us. I like the word *beholding*. It says so much more than *looking*. We need to do more beholding. Keeping a writing journal is the best way I know to practice beholding, seeing life between the lines. Drawing is also wonderful training for seeing beneath the surface.

As we practice the art of beholding, we need to allow our observations to ripen into questions. Without asking our own questions, we will not be able to inspire our children to ask meaningful and probing questions. Our questions open doors to mysteries hidden in the certainties we have come to take for granted. They help us discover the extraordinary in the everyday. They deepen and unfold into new questions that lead us to the heart of understanding the world in us and around us. If we do no more than practice observing and asking questions, our teaching will be transformed.

It was Corina's sixth birthday. It was November, and she had not said a word yet in my kindergarten class. I hoped the occasion might inspire her to let us hear her voice. I encouraged the children to bring a special snack on their birthday. Corina had brought in brownies. Her mother told me that Corina had helped her bake them the night before. "Oh Corina, they are beautiful!" I said. "Will you pass them out at snack time?" She lowered her eyes and nodded her head.

When snack time came, we said a little thank-you verse and sang a special birthday song. "Corina, would you like to pick someone to help you pass out the brownies?" She shook her head. "Okay, I'll help you," I offered.

It was a big moment for Corina. She carried the tray to the first child and lifted it up for him to choose a brownie. "I don't like nuts," Lakeja snapped. My heart sank. Corina guarded her eyes, making sure not to make contact with the next child. Carl chose a brownie, sniffed it, and said, "Yich!" It was a health food kind of brownie, not the soft, gooey, sweet kind. I was fuming as we moved on to the next child. Corina was frozen still. I took a brownie off the tray and gave it to Leonard, hoping to avoid a third trauma. "Hey, I want a bigger one!" he demanded.

Somehow, we made our way around the table. I was appalled at the lack of gratitude in these children. It was my first year of teaching my own class, and I was totally discouraged. How was I going to build gratitude?

I puzzled over the problem that night. I could begin to insist we say please and thank you at every transaction. I could make them hold the door for each other, require other deeds of courtesy. I would surely lecture them about the importance of being thankful for all they had. Thanksgiving was coming soon, so there would be plenty of opportunities to design activities around the idea of giving thanks.

At snack the next morning we returned to our usual fare of graham crackers and apple juice. Even I had to push myself to be thankful for that. Before we eat we always say a little verse in which we thank the earth, the sun, the wind, and the rain for making "ripe the grain." Everyone stood solemnly behind their chair and we said the verse before we sat down. Corina was absent. I was still upset about the previous day, and while we said the verse I was thinking about how I was going to get some gratitude into this obdurate group. Then it hit me. Square in the middle of the heart. Here we were in the one time of the day that I had set aside to express gratitude and what was I doing? Thinking about a problem I was having at work. Here in my one chance to be an example of a person who gives thanks, I was faking it. It was painfully clear to see that before I could ask for gratitude from my students, I had to make it real in myself.

Getting gratitude presented a new problem. How did I get it? It was one thing to recognize that I should have it. It was quite another to make it a real experience in my life. Realizing I should have it was not the same as having it. But I didn't know what to do.

The next morning on the way to school, I turned on the radio to keep me company during the forty-minute commute, but it seemed a distraction. It certainly would not inspire gratitude in my heart. So I turned it off and began to observe the scenery along the route. I drove through some farmland and forest as I approached the city. I was astonished by the tremendous variety of plant life I could observe, even in the late fall. I thought about our verse, and how true it was. I saw the seed as a great conductor of the cosmos, orchestrating the minerals of the earth, the nutrients of the water, the gases of the air, and the energy of the sun. The plant is able to digest these elements and produce its own food, so when I eat a plant I am able to take in the sunlight, the air, the water, and the earth and be refreshed and nourished by them. This was amazing. I began to feel awe and gratitude stirring in my soul. When we said our verse later that morning before snack, I was a different person. I had an authority I did not have before. I was equipped to be the guardian of gratitude. I would let nothing steal it from my class.

When I asked the children to be still, they were still. When I led the verse, they all participated. When one said, "Thank you," the other said, "You're welcome."

I stopped listening to the radio on my way to school. I practiced observation and gratitude. Within two weeks, there was a very different mood in my class. I never had to insist on rules of please and thank you, but we began to hear those words more often. I never had to lecture about all the things we should be thankful for, but we began to show it more. And no matter what else went on during the day, we always had a mood of gratitude when we said our verse before we enjoyed our snack.

I believe the most exciting and effective potential for revitalizing our schools would be to hold ourselves as teachers, individually and collectively, to the same high standards we expect for our children.

Disclaimer

I read a powerful essay recently by Don Murray, who writes an occasional column in the *Boston Globe*. Having trouble composing an opening paragraph, he turned to the works of George Orwell and read the beginnings of many of his essays. He found some extraordinary openers, but what impressed him more were the number of mediocre or even poor beginning paragraphs. He was relieved to realize that he did not have to be George Orwell. In fact, he noted, George Orwell was not even George Orwell most days!

Murray goes on to tell of a friend of his who once played golf with the great Ben Hogan. The friend was surprised to find that at the end of the game his score was quite close to the legendary golfer's. The difference was that after the game Hogan went out and hit four hundred golf balls, a hundred for each of the four shots he'd missed in the game.

Murray realized that what really counted in golf, and in writing, was not the occasional triumph but the habit of working and working and working and being ready for inspiration, as Murray said, "if it happened to pass by."

Working and working and working: a familiar refrain to any teacher. We work hard at the mundane day after day, trying to catch inspiration when it comes by. While many of the stories I tell in this book are the products of such inspirations, I confess that I go home many days pulling my hair out, wondering what I am doing in this business, if I am making any difference at all in these kid's lives. I did not include descriptions of those days in this book. All teachers will have enough examples of their own. I chose to describe instead my attempts to catch the inspiration when it came by. Most days I am not the "Steven Levy" of these inspirations. I offer this confession with the hope of preventing any reader from being discouraged by projects that may seem overwhelmingly complex or by the mistaken impression that my classroom is perpetually filled with a happy teacher and excited, productive children. Although that is of course what I strive for and I rejoice when it actually happens, it doesn't happen every day.

Bibliography

Bradford, W. 1948. *The History of Plymouth Colony.* New York: Van Nostrand.

Emerson, R. W. [1841] 1946. "History." *The Portable Emerson,* ed. Mark Van Doren, 155. New York: The Viking Press.

Gardner, H. 1983. *Frames of Mind: The Theory of Multiple Intelligences.* New York: Basic Books.

Gregor, A. 1965. *Space Pioneer: Galileo Galilei.* New York: Macmillan.

James, T. 1991. "School Principles." Unpublished paper, Education Department, Brown University, Providence, RI.

Macaulay, D. 1983. *The Mill.* Boston: Houghton Mifflin.

McNeer, M., and L. Ward. 1953. *Martin Luther.* New York: Abington Press.

Millstone, D. 1995. *An Elementary Odyssey.* Portsmouth, NH: Heinemann.

Murray, D. 1995. "Like Orwell, Essaying One's Best," *Boston Globe,* January 17.

Postman, N. 1979. *Teaching as a Conserving Activity.* New York: Delacorte.

Postman, N. 1995. *The End of Education: Redefining the Value of School.* New York: Knopf.

Ross, S. 1966. *The English Civil War.* New York: G.P. Putnam's Sons.

Plan for Fourth Grade

Fundamental Principles

We believe learning is a process of development.

Every child is capable of learning in every aspect of education. Every child can be inspired to exercise strengths and work to develop areas of weakness.

We believe in creating an environment that encourages the development and individuality of each child. We believe in providing a wide range of activities: intellectual, artistic, physical, and social, which will give every child an opportunity to demonstrate excellence. When a child has the opportunity to show his or her areas of strength in the class community, he or she will have more confidence and thus be likely to apply more effort in areas of difficulty.

We believe that curriculum begins with observations of the world around us, and then develops through the search for the thoughts, ideas, and origins that give them meaning. It begins with the concrete: what the children see, experience, know, and then proceeds through thought and research to the abstract, to the idea hidden in the phenomenon. This is the heart of our curriculum: observation—questions—research and analysis—sharing results. Curriculum generated by the class in this manner is then guided by the teacher into areas of system-required subject matter.

We believe the curriculum should be integrated by a theme, which permeates and unites all the various areas of study.

Our Plan: How We Would Begin

Our first subject of study would be the classroom environment. We would begin the year with no furniture or supplies. The children would come together and the first order of business would be to anticipate equipment and supplies we would need for the year and design an environment for learning. We would purchase our own supplies and would build the furniture needed for work space and storage with the help of retired carpenters in the community.

For funding we would turn to the Pilgrims for guidance. We study their voyage in the fourth grade social studies curriculum, and how they settled in the new world. How did they fund their journey? They got individuals and businesses to invest. We would re-create their ingenuity and perseverance. We would begin by selling shares in the fourth grade class to local businesses and citizens. Parents would become automatic shareholders. We would sell approximately 40 shares at $50 per share to raise $2000 for our class equipment, supplies and projects. Dividends could be paid in various forms: loaves of Thanksgiving bread from a "farm to table" project, beautiful weavings or hand-knit items from a "sheep to fabric" project; beautiful calendars from a geometric drawing project; paintings and other art projects; free tickets to seasonal concerts of music, poetry, and drama; weekly letters describing activities in class (for parents who never hear from their children what goes on in class, and for citizens who are not aware of what goes on in the schools). A Board of Directors (parents, citizens, students) will be ordained to review class activities and progress and make suggestions.

The price of the original shares would be paid back to the owners at the end of the year after a culminating gala event, at which we serve dinner, entertain, and liquidate all our assets in a raffle. A class museum will be established to display valuable artifacts. These museum pieces (for example, the pencil that John used to get all the spelling words right; the ball Mary kicked the winning goal with; the last leaf on the oak tree we wrote about every month; the picture Peter painted; the poem that Henry wrote in calligraphy; etc.) will also be raffled. Our goal would be to raise enough money to pay back the original amount to the investors. Any additional profit will be used to support school or community needs.

Curriculum

Here are just a few of the curriculum ideas that could arise from such a project:

Math
- Estimating materials needed for the year; how many pencils? etc.
- Accounting and business: planning events, keeping records, setting up a class bank account, allocating funds to different projects, determining profit margins, etc.
- Measurement in furniture design and manufacturing

Science
- Where do the materials we need to use in the class come from? How are they produced? Where? By whom? What effect does that have on our environment?
- Simple machines (4th grade curriculum unit) in tools we use to construct equipment
- How people and animals create spaces for themselves
- Inventions

Social Studies
- We would experience firsthand what the Pilgrims faced in starting from scratch in a new land
- Tremendous opportunity to practice cooperation, compromise, democracy, listening to each other, working together, social skills in a real life context
- The environment: what we use and how we use it

Arts
- Architecture, designing room, decorating: paintings, etc.
- Craft projects
- Study form and composition in music and art

Writing
- Letters to businesses and stockholders
- Persuasive writing

- A history of the progress of our endeavors
- Weekly reports on activities, accomplishments

Responsibility

- Fiscal; we will be self-supportive, motivated by our responsibility to our investors
- Care for materials and equipment; we made them!
- For the group, we all must work together

We will be responsible for all the required curriculum. What we have described here is more of a setting and context through which the curriculum can be more effectively taught.

RATIONALE
Problems We Hope to Address with Our Plan

Curriculum

PROBLEM   The curriculum we are required to teach is vast and fragmented. Each different department (math, science, language arts, social studies, reading, and more recently life skills) has independently developed a curriculum for each grade level. Thus what is taught in one discipline is not related to what is taught in another. Units often come packaged in textbooks or kits. Not only do they lack integration with each other, they often lack relevance to the child's real world.

OUR PLAN   If for no other reason, the economy of time and resources demands we integrate the various subject matter as much as possible. But even more important is the sense of meaning and purpose our children experience when they are led to make connections between what they learn in math and what they learn in social studies; between the methods of conducting a science experiment and the strategies in reading a book. They intuit an intelligent design that stands behind the useful, but abstract, even artificial division of the world into subjects. Even more exciting is when they are able to generate their own curriculum through observations or questions they have about the world! This is really the heart of our self-generated curriculum: observations which provoke questions which inspire research which produces data which requires analysis which leads to con-clusions which demand to be shared. As teachers it is our responsibility (and art) to create an environment in which the children's observations and questions arise in areas of required study. We believe designing a space to live and work in and managing the investments of our stockholders will provide ample opportunities for the development and practice of all basic skills required in the fourth grade curriculum.

We also intend to unite every subject in a common theme. Our theme next year will be rivers. The river itself, with source, banks, current, desti-nation, provides a metaphor for the process of learning itself. It provides a basis for important investigations in geography and history. It is a major reference in our literary heritage, and offers ample material for scientific investigation. It has connections to the system-wide fourth grade curricu-lum, for example the theme of science: change over time, and the social studies theme of settling in a new land. It also connects to the unit on oceans the children will have done in the third grade.

Motivation

PROBLEM   Children need to have some reason to do the work that we expect them to do in school. We reward them for doing their work well and we punish them for neglecting their assignments. Rewards can be in the form of grades, extra privileges, tokens (stickers, candies, small gifts, etc.), or teacher/parent praise. Punishments can be in the form of depriving free time, extra assignments, chastisement, etc. Rewards and punishments are the fuel that runs the train we call motivation. The problem with reward/punishment motivation is: what kind of inner resources does it help to develop in the children? What happens to their desire to learn when you take the popcorn away, when the assignment doesn't get a grade, or alas! if they should get no sticker?

OUR PLAN   Our goal is for the children to be self-motivated. That is, they would find challenge, reward, and enjoyment in the very act of learning itself. This goal is more likely to be realized for each child when they can see the purpose of the work they are given. For example, whereas a child may not see the purpose for filling out worksheets, he or she would see the purpose of estimating how many pencils the class would need for the year, if in fact we were going to actually buy the amount they determine. We want to relate the work we do in class to real life. We want to create a working community that plans for the future and solves real problems. We believe when the work we ask the children to do is related to real life, the children will be motivated from within to apply the full energy of their effort to any task at hand.

Responsibility

PROBLEM   We are alarmed at the lack of responsibility our children show in their actions toward one another and in their care for their environment. The alarming issues of war and environmental devastation we see on a global scale are being played out on a miniature level every day in our classrooms. We are greatly concerned about the lack of respect the children show towards one another, about the way they solve their difficulties and differences. We are equally concerned about their careless use of the materials and resources in the classroom.

OUR PLAN   Our goal is to help develop a sense of responsibility in each child, towards one another and towards the environment. We plan to make our own social life an integral part of our "social studies" lessons, both in relating the dynamics of the classroom to world events current and past, and in taking the time to reflect on our treatment of one another and design strategies to settle our differences. We believe that if the children design the environment themselves, build the work areas and storage spaces, and purchase the equipment and supplies with funds from their own class treasury, then they will quite naturally show greater responsibility in taking care of it.

Parent Involvement

PROBLEM   The education of the children is ultimately the responsibility of the parents. The schools exist to help them in this formidable task. But too often parents lack access to the educational process in the classroom. They do not have ample opportunity to communicate their family values, their goals for their children to the teacher. The teacher does not have a way to communicate to the parents what is happening in class, and the children don't talk about it.

OUR PLAN   The children are the most secure when they sense that their teachers and parents are in this business together. We will make every effort to make this possible. First, we will visit each family over the summer to meet the children and hear the goals of the parents. We will conduct class evenings throughout the year in which we report on class events and hear ideas, concerns, and feedback from the parents. We will invite parents to four seasonal festivals of music, poetry, recorder playing, dance, and display of work. Parents, as shareholders, will get weekly dividends: written reports from the children about the events of the week.

Community Involvement

PROBLEM   Our school often operates in isolation. The part of the community that has no children in the system sees the schools as a drain on the town's limited financial resources. Other resources that the community has are not utilized by the school.

OUR PLAN   The health of the school ultimately depends on the support of the community. We intend to involve the community by giving citizens the opportunity to purchase shares in the class. We will choose a Board of Directors from community and parent members who will review the activities of the class and make recommendations. All community shareholders will receive weekly reports of class activities, and free tickets to all concerts, plays, and special events. They will also receive the fruits of class projects, such as a loaf of bread from our "Farm to Table" project, a weaving from our "Sheep to Cloth" project, a calendar from our geometric drawing, etc. We also plan to invite retired citizens to work with us in different ways in the class.

Faculty Meeting Questions

June 16, 1992
To: The Faculty
From: Steven
Re: Some questions raised at faculty meeting June 15

1. What if no fifth grade teacher wants to move to fourth grade in 1993?

Response: Although we feel that spending two years with a class is a benefit to the children, we are not asking that anyone be reassigned involuntarily. If no fifth grade teacher is interested, we will do what we can in one year.

2. What about parents who cannot afford to buy a share?

Response: We do not want to put parents in a position in which they feel obliged to buy a share. We would offer two kinds of shares, one for parents of the class which would be free. These shares will entitle parents to all of the dividends described in the proposal. A second kind of share would be made available for purchase by community members and businesses.

3. How will you have time to teach the curriculum?

Response: We are responsible for teaching the curriculum and preparing students for fifth grade and beyond. What we are describing is not a replacement for the curriculum, but rather a context in which to teach it that will provide integration, meaning and motivation.

4. Aren't you making these children junior capitalists?

Response: Our society is built on capitalism. The enemy we are seeking to avoid is not an economic system, but human greed. In our current system, the children take much that is given to them for granted. Their treatment of materials and equipment shows it. I believe that by making concrete the resources that it takes to run a classroom, and letting the children play a role in raising funds and allocating them, they will be much more responsible in managing and caring for their environment. Furthermore, a first-hand experience of how our economy works will be a valuable lesson for life. Our goal is not to make profits. If we raise more money than we need to operate our classroom, we will have the joy of helping others in the school or town with a contribution.

5. How can you justify buying more furniture when we have so much already? Shouldn't we be teaching recycling?

Response: After our needs have been determined, the first place we would look is our own "backyard." If the school has things that we need, we would be happy to use them. But it is important for the children to recognize the need first, then look for ways to fulfill it. As was stated above, I believe this plan would engender a much higher level of appreciation and care for the resources we use. Indeed, part of the curriculum plan is to study the origin of all the materials we use in the classroom and the impact of manufacturing these materials on the environment.

6. We shouldn't be doing research on a child in the class.

Response: We presented this part of the plan poorly. All we meant was that we wanted to observe a special needs student carefully, adjust the program to meet his needs, and document his progress.

7. What about the noise you will make?

Response: We would plan to do any building outside or at times when our neighbors have special subjects outside their classroom. We wouldn't build anything on rainy days.

8. What if there are parents who are not supportive?

Response: We will present the plan to the parents as soon as they are notified of their child's placement. We will present it as an idea we are thinking about and solicit their input. If they don't like the idea we wouldn't do it. If there are one or two parents who don't like it, I don't think we would be different from any other class in that respect. They will have to adapt. If the program goes for two years, they can transfer after the first.

9. Won't you be isolated from the rest of the faculty?

Response: This is a very important question for Debbie and me personally, and for us as a faculty. Does doing something different from your neighbors have to isolate you from them? One of our goals as a community is multiculturalism and respect for diversity. We want the children to respect differences, to try to learn what motivates another, to be interested in how someone else thinks and why they act the way they do. Can we expect less from ourselves? Whenever any individual in a community wants to do something different, it is a challenge to the individual and the community. The individual must examine his or her motives. The community must examine its resistance. We have to work this out together. So whether or not this plan would isolate us from the community is up to all of us. It is a challenge. But not to pursue the idea because it is different represents a dangerous threat to our faculty and a message to the children I am sure we do not want to deliver.

Desk Olympics Events

Deskolympics '93
Events: sign up for 3

1. desk limbo   Katrina, Peretz, Becky, Liza, Chloe, Rachel
2. homework excuse   Katie, Noah, Allie
3. seed separater   Martin, Chloe
4. fastest drill in the East
5. push-pull contest   Chris, Toby, Katie, Allie, Jeremy, Emeka, Zarmon, Peretz
6. hat toss   Emeka, Leah, Zarmon
7. funniest face   Martin, Luke, Evan
8. stick jump   Evan, Chris
9. saw contest
10. backwards count
11. pulley contest   Matthew, Martin, Katie, Noah, Luke, Katrina, Chloe, Siobhan, Liza, Becky
    17.4   25.6   16.5 10.0 21.8 17.5 9.8 13.0   9.7
12. mr. Levy impersonation   Noah, Rachel, Katrina, Leah, Liza, Becky
13. ~~football fling~~   airplane toss — Matthew, Victor, Toby, Jeremy, Luke.
14. best joke
15. pillow challenge   Matthew, Chris, Victor, Toby, Rachel, Jeremy, Leah, Evan, Siobhan, Peretz
16. wastebasket ball   Allie, Emeka, Zarmon

Pilgrims '92 Class Poem

Pilgrims '92, The Year in Review

Parents and shareholders, have no fear
Pilgrims '92 is here.   SL

The Pilgrims ninety-two and three
Had a very fine year as you can see.
We began in September without desks or chairs
'Til our valued investors purchased their shares.   ALL

At first we sat upon the floor
But now we sit on chairs galore.   BR

The first day of school the floor was bare
But now we have desks and room to spare.   KU

We dug and plowed and dug some more
Until our hands were raw and sore.
We added farmer's gold to the plot
To help our seeds to grow a lot.
We then threw berries on the ground
'Til they were scattered all around.
We learned the names and parts of the wheat
And the berries grew through snow and sleet.
Our wheat is tall, the stalks are gold

And almost ripe, so we are told.
The class enjoyed the planting stuff
Even though it was kind of rough.   EE

The first day of school when we entered the room
We suddenly noticed a great big loom.
We learned to weave and we weaved some more
Making scarves and rugs to cover the floor.   KS

From raw wool we made some string
For bags and scarves for us to bring
Home to our parents and to share tonight
We think they make a lovely sight.   NE

We made knitting needles to go click, click;
Some scarves are long and some are thick.
We knitted 'til our hands did ache
And then we stopped to take a break.   AS

Then we commenced mathematical actions
While setting our minds on those worrisome fractions. LF

In reading we read lots of books
And learned to judge them not by looks.   VC

Creative writing is so much fun.
You can be most anyone!   MW

When the day showed dreary gloom
We wrote about it in our room.
When on a sunny day we looked,
We wrote about it in our book.   LD

In the morning on the floor, electricity galore.
In the filament there was a fight, between the darkness and the light. LB

Galileo was so good
He wrote books I understood.

He made people plenty mad
And that got me so very glad.   ZM

We learned about Pilgrims way back then
And how they kept their pigs in a pen.   PD

We worked so hard on our newsletter
We hope you think it couldn't be better.   AK

I look at the river rushing by
At the leaves floating quickly, I wonder why
The current smooths the rocks on its way
From the source, a spring, to the mouth, a bay.   JS

In Spanish we learned our words so well.
One is "campana," which means a bell.   KW

Mr. Rick was the best
In all the students he did invest
So much time and so much care
So much of himself he did share.
Each of us in room number 9
Feel that Mr. Rick is really fine.
He helped us out with games and math
And all the while he made us laugh.
When I think of him most of all
I remember playing basketball.
And now he's gone in Yellowstone,
To the buffaloes, Mr. Rick, we must loan.   EL

Ms. Hart she made us body smart
She taught about our bones and heart.   KW

Ms. Rader left a dream catcher with maple syrup sweet.
She taught us all a river song with a really rhythmic beat.   SL

Ms. O'Hara taught us dances and twirls
When we moved around our clothes made swirls.   AK

Pilgrims '92 Class Poem

We memorized each lovely song
Even though it took us long.
We sang until our show-time came
Our singing is our claim to fame.   CS

On recorders we keep the beat
And that is really very neat.
Our teachers made us memorize
Until we all could harmonize.   PD

Our performances are so great,
By far the best in our whole state.   TLE

Mrs. Butler brought her camera in,
And we hope our video gives you a grin.   CO

The investors of Pilgrims ninety-two and three
Were very kind as you can see.
We are very grateful to one and all
You did not let us take a fall.
We feel that we must let you know
We are very sorry to see you go.   RJ

Directions for "Number" Drawings

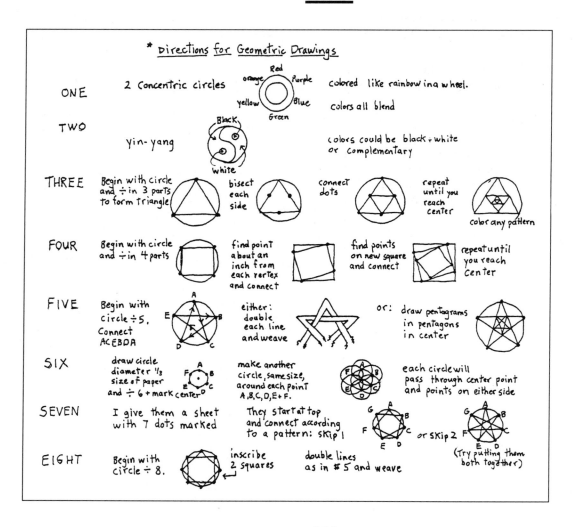

* Directions for Geometric Drawings

ONE — 2 Concentric circles — colored like rainbow in a wheel. colors all blend

Red, Purple, Blue, Green, Yellow, orange

TWO — yin-yang — colors could be black + white or complementary

Black, white

THREE — Begin with circle and ÷ in 3 parts to form Triangle — bisect each side — connect dots — repeat until you reach center — color any pattern

FOUR — Begin with circle and ÷ in 4 parts — find point about an inch from each vertex and connect — find points on new square and connect — repeat until you reach center

FIVE — Begin with circle ÷ 5, Connect ACEBDA — either: double each line and weave — or: draw pentagrams in pentagons in center

SIX — draw circle diameter ⅓ size of paper and ÷ 6 + mark center — make another circle, same size, around each point A, B, C, D, E + F. — each circle will pass through center point and points on either side

SEVEN — I give them a sheet with 7 dots marked — They start at top and connect according to a pattern: skip 1 — or skip 2 — (Try putting them both together)

EIGHT — Begin with circle ÷ 8. — inscribe 2 squares — double lines as in #5 and weave

NINE   same as 7

TEN   Begin with circle ÷ 10   inscribe pentagram ←   start to inscribe 2nd pentagram but stop when you reach a line   erase pentagon in center

ELEVEN   I give sheet with 11 dots   connect A to every dot / connect B to every dot

A B

TWELVE   I give them sheet with 12 dots   connect every dot to every dot / I let them use ruler on this one

★ You could, of course, make up your own! We do all drawings freehand (except 12)

Original Bike-Path Questions

History

What happened to the railroads? Why did the railroads end? What did they do with the old trains and tracks? Were there any robberies on the train? How was Lexington affected when the railroad closed? Did the trains carry cargo or people? Did people bike before they rode in cars? How did they get help if they got hurt and there were no ambulances? Did cars ever go on the land where the path is? Why did they build the train track where they did? What was there before the trains?

Planning

What gave people the idea of a bike path? Who were the first planners? Why is the path where it is? How did they decide how long to make it? Why did they decide a bike path and not something else like a road or trolley or subway? Why was a bike path better than a railroad? Were there any other ideas people had besides a bike path? Were there people against the plan? Why? Are there any plans for future development?

Construction

How long did it take to build the path? How many kinds of workers and how many workers did it take? What equipment was needed? What is pavement? What kind is best?

Users

Any problems between different users, like Rollerbladers, walkers, etc.? How do people compare riding on streets to riding on the path? Did anyone ride on the dirt before it was a bike path? Can you do tricks like jumps and stuff? How many people use the bike path?

Abutters

How many people live next to the bike path? How many businesses? Can we find out who they are? How do they feel about the path? Did their opinion about the bike path change after it was built? Do people who use the path cause any trouble for the abutters, like ride on their property, litter, make noise, etc.?

Business

Is the bike path good or bad for business? What kind of businesses are helped most? Who owned the land? Who owns the bike path? Were companies like utilities affected? What companies ran the trains? Did they go out of business or something else? Did people use the trains to get to work?

Environment

How does the path affect animals? Was there any environmental reason for building the bike path? How did the bike path affect plants? Are any plants that used to be there gone? Are there any new ones? Any animals killed? Why are there places of erosion?

Safety

Have there been any animal attacks? Any rabid animals? Have there been any deaths or injuries? Are there any dangerous places? Where? When will they get the bullies off the path? What is done so people don't get hit by cars at intersections? Were there more accidents before or after the bike path? What kind of signs are on the bike path? Who makes them? How did there come to be police bike riders? Why fences? Why locks? Who has the key?

197

Costs

How much did it cost to build? Were there other costs beside the pavement? Who paid for it? Are there any continuing ongoing costs? Taxes? Maintenance? How much did it cost to pay workers? Did they all get the same amount? How much for materials?

The Bicycle

What was the first bicycle? What kinds of changes made it easier to ride? Is a bicycle better than a horse? What is the future of the bicycle?

Interpreting Bike-Path Data

NAME A: Ian
       B: Margaret

STREET Maple

KEY

J Joggers | Bikes
· Walkers
B Baby Carriages   Ignore E
R Rollerblades, Rollerskates

Time	TO ARLINGTON (EAST)	TO BEDFORD (WEST)
4:00–4:15	RR │ ┼ · ││││ ✓	│ R IE BE IR · · · J J ││ ✓
4:15–4:30	┼┼┼ R · │ J · ││ R │ E┼ ✓	Ⓔₜₜ ┼┼┼ │. · J R · ││││ · · R ✓
4:30–4:45	· ·· │ · · · │ RR ││.E│ ⁄││ │ │ ✓	RB ┼┼┼ RR │ R ⁄⁄⁄│ ┼ IE ││ IE ⁄.E IE ✓
4:45–5:00	││││ · · · BR │ ⁄ │ │ │ ││ │ J ✓	R J ││ · Ⓔ IE │ R J IE IE · ⁄│ IE ✓
5:00–5:15	R J J · · RR ⁄⁄ RE · ✓	││ B │ J ✓
5:15–5:30	R · ⁄ │ │ J E BE R: ✓	│ │ │ ⁄⁄ RE │ │ ││ │ │ J ⒾⒺ ⁄⁄ ⒾⒺ │ │ ││ │
5:30–5:45	│ ⁄ R ⁄⁄ Ⓔ · ⁄⁄ R ││ JE ⁄ RR R J J J │ R ││││ ⒾⒺ	J ⁄E ⁄⁄ ⒾⒺ · │ RR R ⁄⁄ IE⁄ R ││ · │││ \ .. ⁄⁄ RR │ RR
5:45–6:00	││ R · · E⁄ · J⁄ ⁄⁄ R ⁄ │ ⁄⁄	R IR │ │ · E R ⁄ │ ⁄⁄ IE RR RE ⁄ │⁄

199

Margaret, Ian, Serina   Sarah. Izen
counters name ?   your name ?

Maple
street ?

Time	To Arlington (East)						To Bedford (west)					
	1	J	.	R	B	other	1	J	.	R	B	other
4:00 - 4:15	6	0	1	2	0	0	5	2	3	2	1	0
4:15 - 4:30	9	1	2	2	0	0	9	1	9	2	0	0
4:30 - 4:45	10	0	6	2	0	0	16	0	1	4	0	0
4:45 - 5:00	17	1	4	1	1	0	11	2	3	2	0	0
5:00 - 5:15	2	2	3	4	0	0	3	1	2	1	0	0
5:15 - 5:30	3	1	2	2	1	0	16	1	1	1	0	0
5:30 - 5:45	17	4	1	6	0	0	19	1	4	8	0	0
5:45 - 6:00	10	1	3	1	0	0	11	0	1	6	0	0
6:00 - 6:15	17	3	1	4	0	0	15	4	0	1	0	0
6:15 - 6:30	12	3	0	4	0	0	9	3	1	6	1	0
TOTALS	103	16	23	28	2	0	114	15	25	33	2	0

Do you see any patterns? **not really** what do we learn from this data? I learned that more people where going to bedford

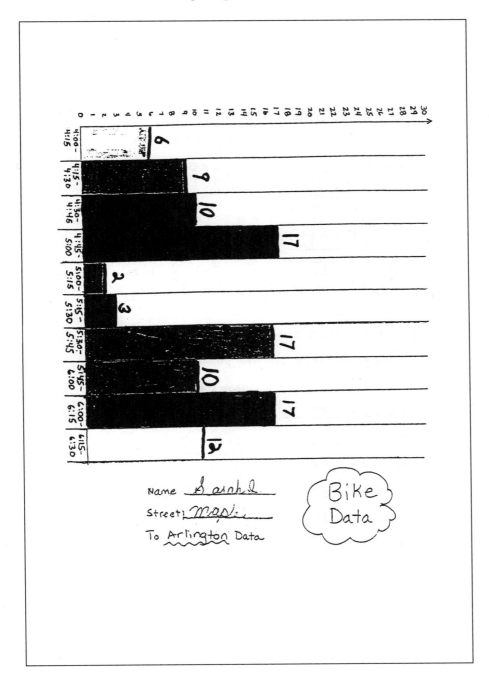

Name _S arnh l_
Street: _man_
To _Arlington_ Data

Bike
Data

Name *Serena*   MAPLE STREET DATA

1. What was the _total_ number of bikes on the path at :

show your work :

4:00 – 4:15	11	6 + 5 = 11
4:15 – 4:30	18	9 + 9 = 18
4:30 – 4:45	26	10 + 16 = 26
4:45 – 5:00	28	17 + 11 = 28
5:00 – 5:15	5	2 + 3 = 5
5:15 – 5:30	19	3 + 16 = 19
5:30 – 5:45	36	17 + 18 = 36
5:45 – 6:00	21	10 + 11 = 21
6:00 – 6:15	32	17 + 15 = 32
6:15 – 6:30	21	12 + 9 = 21

2. Using the numbers above ↑, what was the _total_ number of bikes on the path at :

show your work:

4:00 – 5:00	83	11 + 18 + 26 + 28 = 83
4:15 – 5:15	77	18 + 26 + 28 + 5 = 77
4:30 – 5:30	78	26 + 28 + 5 + 19 = 78
4:45 – 5:45	88	28 + 5 + 19 + 36 = 88
5:00 – 6:00	81	5 + 19 + 36 + 21 = 81
5:15 – 6:15	108	19 + 36 + 21 + 32 = 108
5:30 – 6:30	110	36 + 21 + 32 + 21 = 110

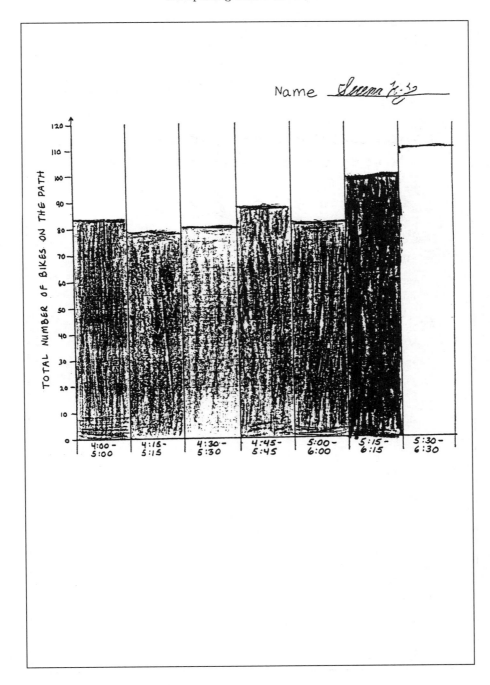

Name _____

1. What was the peak hour for
   bicycles (East + West) on the bike
   path?

   $5:30 - 6:30 = 110$

2. What was the total number of
   bicycles on the path during
   that peak hour?

   110

The Challenge !   Johnny
                     name

spring
Look at data sheets together and discuss any interesting
similarities or differences or patterns.

more bikes than enything else.

more users are going to arlington.
not many users use the bike
path at 4:30 – 5:00.
speeds up from 5:15 – 6:00.
baby carridges and other have no users.

2. *spring + fall*
   Compare the Spring data to the Fall data. Again, look
   for similarities, differences or patterns.

   more bikes going to arlington
   in the spring.

   move baby caridges and other
   in the fall.

   more roler bladeing in the spring
   going to arlington.

3. Based on your observations, what are some questions
   the data suggests to you ?

1. why are more users going to arlington
2. why do more users use the path
in the spring?
3. why is it slow from 4:30 – 5:00

PUBLIC LIBR...
...SON COUNTY
LIBRARY SYSTEM

DISCARD - WEEDED

LIBRARY SYSTEM